An Ethics of Sexual Difference

This volume continues and completes Irigaray's writing on 'sexual difference' by addressing the ethical implications of her work. Irigaray speaks out against the egalitarian project of feminism important to the Anglo-American school of women thinkers and pursues questions of sexual difference, arguing that all thought and language is gendered and that there can therefore be no neutral thought—in philosophy, science or psychoanalysis.

The author
Luce Irigaray (CNRS, Paris) is a leading philosopher and thinker in the field of feminist ideas. Already published by Athlone is *Elemental Passions,* and forthcoming are *A Time for Difference: For a Peaceful Revolution* (1993) and *Speech Is Never Neuter* (1994).

LUCE IRIGARAY

An Ethics of Sexual Difference

TRANSLATED FROM THE FRENCH BY

Carolyn Burke and Gillian C. Gill

The Athlone Press

London

First published in Great Britain in 1993 by
The Athlone Press Ltd
1 Park Drive, London, NW11 7SG

First published in France in 1984 by
Les Editions de Minuit, Paris as
Éthique de la Différence Sexuelle

Publisher's Note
The publishers wish to record their thanks to the
French Ministry of Culture for a grant towards
the cost of translation.

British Library Cataloguing in Publication Data
*A catalogue record for this book is available
from the British Library*

ISBN 0 485 30067 2 hb
         0 485 30070 2 pb

Typeset by The Composing Room of Michigan, Inc.
Printed and bound by Thomson-Shore, Inc.

Contents

Contents

Translators' Note

The task of Irigaray's translator is not to eliminate ambiguities and difficulties but to produce a text that is no more—and no less—challenging than the original. For example, because Irigaray likes to create new forms of words, readers of this book will occasionally find terms that do not exist in any English dictionary—or in any French one. She sometimes uses words from ancient Greek, such as *polemos, aesthesis, hypokeimenon, morphé,* and *apatheia;* some of these terms are more familiar than others, and some (such as *polemos*) are used in a non-standard sense. We have, however, resisted the urge to translate them because we trust that, on the whole, the English reader, like the French reader, is more likely to enter into Irigaray's way of thinking by tracing the etymologies of such terms while attending to the contexts in which they appear in her work. Even more challenging is the way she habitually incorporates into her own prose terms from the philosophical texts she is reading. This technique of *mimétisme,* carefully set out in *Speculum of the Other Woman* and *This Sex Which Is Not One,* should not, however, be construed to mean that Irigaray is necessarily adopting or assenting to the words and ideas she echoes.

Other lexical idiosyncrasies result from the fact that we have carried forward into this translation specific words and expressions used in the philosophical texts she is analyzing—as they have been rendered in the standard English translations. Thus, in "Place, Interval," the unexceptional French *transport* has been rendered as *locomotion* not because we like this word but because it is used in the translation which we cite.

Finally, because typography and format are such significant elements in the Irigarayan text, we have sought not to standardize idiosyncratic usage but rather to respect her deliberate deviations from editorial norms wherever possible. Thus, as in the French edition, extra spacing is often used to mark pauses for reflection, stages in the unfolding of the argument, or parallelisms in the marshaling of examples in support of a thesis. Again, as in the French, italics are frequently used for those passages which do not simply quote her interlocutors but make them present as partners in a philosophical dialogue—as the other voices against and with which Irigaray sets her own. We have respected these practices because we believe that it is only when Irigaray's readers engage with her textuality that they fully experience what she is "saying."

C. B. AND G. C. G.

An Ethics of Sexual Difference

This collection consists of lectures given at Erasmus University in Rotterdam. They were delivered under the provisions of the Jan Tinbergen Chair, which is occupied for one semester each year by a foreign researcher; it was awarded to me in philosophy for the second semester of 1982. It is understood that whoever holds this chair will do original work in connection with his or her already published research and leave some written record of it.

Course work was condensed into four months. Each month there was a lecture followed by discussion (discussions are not reproduced here). On the following day, two reading seminars on philosophical texts were held. The lectures and readings appear in this book in chronological order. Other more varied activities—students' presentations of their current work, discussions, and so on—are not reproduced here.

Traditionally, a lecture addressed to the university teaching staff and open to the public and, of course, to the students is included in this program. That lecture, given November 18, 1982, has already been published in a small bilingual volume by the University of Rotterdam and is reproduced here under the title "An Ethics of Sexual Difference."

I am grateful to the Dutch women who invited me to Rotterdam, the Department of Women's Studies, Professor Kimmerle, and all those who welcomed me at Erasmus University, especially Agnès Manschot Vincenot, who saw to the translation of the lectures into Dutch.

[1]

I pay homage to the work of Jan Tinbergen, whose efforts made possible the creation of this international chair, which I occupied in philosophy in order to speak about "The Ethics of the Passions."

L. I.

I

Sexual Difference

Sexual difference is one of the major philosophical issues, if not the issue, of our age. According to Heidegger, each age has one issue to think through, and one only. Sexual difference is probably the issue in our time which could be our "salvation" if we thought it through.

But, whether I turn to philosophy, to science, or to religion, I find this underlying issue still cries out in vain for our attention. Think of it as an approach that would allow us to check the many forms that destruction takes in our world, to counteract a nihilism that merely affirms the reversal or the repetitive proliferation of status quo values—whether you call them the consumer society, the circularity of discourse, the more or less cancerous diseases of our age, the unreliability of words, the end of philosophy, religious despair or regression to religiosity, scientistic or technical imperialism that fails to consider the living subject.

Sexual difference would constitute the horizon of worlds more fecund than any known to date—at least in the West—and without reducing fecundity to the reproduction of bodies and flesh. For loving partners this would be a fecundity of birth and regeneration, but also the production of a new age of thought, art, poetry, and language: the creation of a new *poetics*.

Both in theory and in practice, everything resists the discovery and affirmation of such an advent or event. In theory, philosophy wants to be literature or rhetoric, wishing either to break with ontology or to regress to the ontological. Using the same ground and the same framework as "first philosophy," working toward its disintegration but without proposing any other goals that might assure new foundations and new works.

In politics, some overtures have been made to the world of women. But these overtures remain partial and local: some concessions have been made by those in power, but no new values have been established. Rarely have these measures been thought through and affirmed by women themselves, who consequently remain at the level of critical demands. Has a worldwide erosion of the gains won in women's struggles occurred because of the failure to lay foundations different from those on which the world of men is constructed? Psychoanalytic theory and therapy, the scenes of sexuality as such, are a long way from having effected their revolution. And with a few exceptions, sexual practice today is often divided between two parallel worlds: the world of men and the world of women. A nontraditional, fecund encounter between the sexes barely exists. It does not voice its demands publicly, except through certain kinds of silence and polemics.

A revolution in thought and ethics is needed if the work of sexual difference is to take place. We need to reinterpret everything concerning the relations between the subject and discourse, the subject and the world, the subject and the cosmic, the microcosmic and the macrocosmic. Everything, beginning with the way in which the subject has always been written in the masculine form, as *man*, even when it claimed to be universal or neutral. Despite the fact that *man*—at least in French—rather than being neutral, is sexed.

Man has been the subject of discourse, whether in theory, morality, or politics. And the gender of God, the guardian of every subject and every discourse, is always *masculine and pater-*

[6]

nal, in the West. To women are left the so-called minor arts: cooking, knitting, embroidery, and sewing; and, in exceptional cases, poetry, painting, and music. Whatever their importance, these arts do not currently make the rules, at least not overtly.

Of course, we are witnessing a certain reversal of values: manual labor and art are being revalued. But the relation of these arts to sexual difference is never really thought through and properly apportioned. At best, it is related to the class struggle.

In order to make it possible to think through, and live, this difference, we must reconsider the whole problematic of *space* and *time*.

In the beginning there was space and the creation of space, as is said in all theogonies. The gods, God, first create *space*. And time is there, more or less in the service of space. On the first day, the first days, the gods, God, make a world by separating the elements. This world is then peopled, and a rhythm is established among its inhabitants. God would be time itself, lavishing or exteriorizing itself in its action in space, in places.

Philosophy then confirms the genealogy of the task of the gods or God. Time becomes the *interiority* of the subject itself, and space, its *exteriority* (this problematic is developed by Kant in the *Critique of Pure Reason*). The subject, the master of time, becomes the axis of the world's ordering, with its something beyond the moment and eternity: God. He effects the passage between time and space.

Which would be inverted in sexual difference? Where the feminine is experienced as space, but often with connotations of the abyss and night (God being space and light?), while the masculine is experienced as time.

The transition to a new age requires a change in our perception and conception of *space-time*, the inhabiting of places, and of containers, or envelopes of identity. It assumes and entails an evolution or a transformation of forms, of the relations of *matter* and *form* and of the interval *between*: the trilogy of the constitution of

[7]

place. Each age inscribes a limit to this trinitary configuration: *matter, form, interval,* or *power* [*puissance*]*, act, intermediary-interval*.

Desire occupies or designates the place of the *interval*. Giving it a permanent definition would amount to suppressing it as desire. Desire demands a sense of attraction: a change in the interval, the displacement of the subject or of the object in their relations of nearness or distance.

The transition to a new age comes at the same time as a change in the economy of desire. A new age signifies a different relation between:

— man and god(s),
— man and man,
— man and world,
— man and woman.

Our age, which is often thought to be one in which the problematic of desire has been brought forward, frequently theorizes this desire on the basis of observations of a moment of tension, or a moment in history, whereas desire ought to be thought of as a changing dynamic whose outlines can be described in the past, sometimes in the present, but never definitively predicted. Our age will have failed to realize the full dynamic reserve signified by desire if it is referred back to the economy of the *interval*, if it is situated in the attractions, tensions, and actions occurring between *form* and *matter*, but also in the *remainder* that subsists after each creation or work, *between* what has already been identified and what has still to be identified, and so on.

In order to imagine such an economy of desire, one must reinterpret what Freud implies by *sublimation* and observe that he does not speak of the sublimation of genitality (except in reproduction? But, if this were a successful form of sublimation, Freud would not be so pessimistic about parental child-rearing practices) or of the sublimation of the *partial drives in relation to the feminine* but rather of their repression (little girls speak earlier and more skillfully than little boys; they have a better relationship to the social; and so on—qualities or aptitudes that disappear without leaving any creative achievements that capitalize on their energy, except for the task of becoming a woman: an object of attraction?)[1]

In this possible nonsublimation of herself, and by herself, woman always tends *toward* without any return to herself as the place where something positive can be elaborated. In terms of contemporary physics, it could be said that she remains on the side of the electron, with all that this implies for her, for man, for their encounter. If there is no double desire, the positive and negative poles divide themselves between the two sexes instead of establishing a chiasmus or a double loop in which each can go toward the other and come back to itself.

If these positive and negative poles are not found in both, the same one always attracts, while the other remains in motion but lacks a "proper" place. What is missing is the double pole of attraction and support, which excludes disintegration or rejection, attraction and decomposition, but which instead ensures the separation that articulates every encounter and makes possible speech, promises, alliances.

In order to distance oneself, must one be able to take? To speak? Which in a certain way comes to the same thing. Perhaps in order to take, one needs a fixed container or place? A soul? Or a spirit? Mourning nothing is the most difficult. Mourning the self in the other is almost impossible. I search for myself, as if I had been assimilated into maleness. I ought to reconstitute myself on the basis of a disassimilation. . . .[2] Rise again from the traces of a culture, of works already produced by the other. Searching through what is in them—for what is not there. What

---

[1] Cf. Luce Irigaray, *Speculum, de l'autre femme* (Paris: Minuit, 1984), pp. 9–162; trans. Gillian C. Gill, under the title *Speculum of the Other Woman* (Ithaca: Cornell University Press, 1985), pp. 11–129.

[2] (All ellipses occur in the original French text and do not indicate omissions in the translation.—Tr.)

allowed them to be, for what is not there. Their conditions of possibility, for what is not there.

Woman ought to be able to find herself, among other things, through the images of herself already deposited in history and the conditions of production of the work of man, and not on the basis of his work, his genealogy.

If traditionally, and as a mother, woman represents *place* for man, such a limit means that she becomes *a thing*, with some possibility of change from one historical period to another. She finds herself delineated as a thing. Moreover, the maternal-feminine also serves as an *envelope*, a *container*, the starting point from which man limits his things. The *relationship between envelope and things* constitutes one of the aporias, or the aporia, of Aristotelianism and of the philosophical systems derived from it.

In our terminologies, which derive from this economy of thought but are impregnated with a psychologism unaware of its sources, it is said, for example, that the woman-mother is *castrating*. Which means that, since her status as envelope and as thing(s) has not been interpreted, she remains inseparable from the work or act of man, notably insofar as he defines her and creates *his* identity with her as his starting point or, correlatively, with this determination of her being. If after all this, she is still alive, she continuously undoes his work—distinguishing herself from both the envelope and the thing, ceaselessly creating there some interval, play, something in motion and un-limited which disturbs his perspective, his world, and his/its limits. But, because he fails to leave her a subjective life, and to be on occasion her place and her thing in an intersubjective dynamic, man remains within a master-slave dialectic. The slave, ultimately, of a God on whom he bestows the characteristics of an absolute master. Secretly or obscurely, a slave to the power of the maternal-feminine which he diminishes or destroys.

The maternal-feminine remains the *place separated from "its" own place*, deprived of "its" place. She is or ceaselessly becomes the place of the other who cannot separate himself from it.

Without her knowing or willing it, she is then threatening because of what she lacks: a "proper" place. She would have to
re-envelop herself with herself, and do so at least twice: as a
woman and as a mother. Which would presuppose a change in
the whole economy of space-time.

In the meantime, this ethical question comes into play in matters of *nudity* and *perversity*. Woman must be nude because she is
not situated, does not situate herself in her place. Her clothes,
her makeup, and her jewels are the things with which she tries
to create her container(s), her envelope(s). She cannot make use
of the envelope that she is, and must create artificial ones.

Freud's statement that woman is identified with orality is
meaningful, but it still exiles her from her most archaic and
constituent site. No doubt orality is an especially significant
measure for her: morphologically, she has two mouths and two
pairs of lips. But she can act on this morphology or make something of it only if she preserves her relation to *spatiality* and to
the *fetal*. Although she needs these dimensions to create a space
for herself (as well as to maintain a receptive place for the other),
they are traditionally taken from her to constitute man's nostalgia and everything that he constructs in memory of this first
and ultimate dwelling place. An obscure commemoration. . . .
Centuries will perhaps have been needed for man to interpret the
meaning of his work(s): the endless construction of a number of
substitutes for his prenatal home. From the depths of the earth
to the highest skies? Again and again, taking from the feminine
the tissue or texture of spatiality. In exchange—but it isn't a real
one—he buys her a house, even shuts her up in it, places limits
on her that are the opposite of the unlimited site in which he
unwittingly situates her. He contains or envelops her with walls
while enveloping himself and his things with her flesh. The
nature of these envelopes is not the same: on the one hand,
invisibly alive, but with barely perceivable limits; on the other,
visibly limiting or sheltering, but at the risk of being prison-like
or murderous if the threshold is not left open.

We must, therefore, reconsider the whole question of our

conception of place, both in order to move on to another age of difference (each age of thought corresponds to a particular time of meditation on difference), and in order to construct an ethics of the passions. We need to change the relations between form, matter, interval, and limit, an issue that has never been considered in a way that allows for a relationship between two loving subjects of different sexes.

Once there was the enveloping body and the enveloped body, the latter being the more mobile through what Aristotle termed *locomotion* (since maternity does not look much like "motion"). The one who offers or allows desire moves and envelops, engulfing the other. It is moreover a danger if no third term exists. Not only to serve as a limitation. This third term can occur within the one who contains as a relation of the latter to his or her own limit(s): relation to the divine, to death, to the social, to the cosmic. If a third term does not exist within and for the container, he or she becomes *all-powerful*.

Therefore, to deprive one pole of sexual difference, women, of a third term also amounts to putting them in the position of omnipotence: this is a danger for men, especially in that it suppresses an interval that is both entrance and space between.[3] A place for both to enter and exit the envelope (and on the same side, so as not to perforate the envelope or assimilate it into the digestive process); for both, a possibility of unhindered movement, of peaceful immobility without the risk of imprisonment.

To arrive at the constitution of an ethics of sexual difference, we must at least return to what is for Descartes the first passion: *wonder*. This passion has no opposite or contradiction and exists always as though for the first time. Thus man and woman,

---

[3] (Irigaray plays on the double sense of *entre*, meaning both "enter" and "between."—Tr.)

woman and man are always meeting as though for the first time because they cannot be substituted one for the other. I will never be in a man's place, never will a man be in mine. Whatever identifications are possible, one will never exactly occupy the place of the other—they are irreducible one to the other.

"*When the first encounter with some object surprises us, and we judge it to be new, or very different from what we formerly knew, or from what we supposed that it ought to be, that causes us to wonder and be surprised; and because that may happen before we in any way know whether this object is agreeable to us or is not so, it appears to me that wonder is the first of all the passions; and it has no opposite, because if the object which presents itself has nothing in it that surprises us, we are in nowise moved regarding it, and we consider it without passion.*" (René Descartes, *The Passions of the Soul*, article 53).[4]

Who or what the other is, I never know. But the other who is forever unknowable is the one who differs from me sexually. This feeling of surprise, astonishment, and wonder in the face of the unknowable ought to be returned to its locus: that of sexual difference. The passions have either been repressed, stifled, or reduced, or reserved for God. Sometimes a space for wonder is left to works of art. But it is never found to reside in this locus: *between man and woman*. Into this place came attraction, greed, possession, consummation, disgust, and so on. But not that wonder which beholds what it sees always as if for the first time, never taking hold of the other as its object. It does not try to seize, possess, or reduce this object, but leaves it subjective, still free.

This has never existed between the sexes since wonder maintains their autonomy within their statutory difference, keeping a space of freedom and attraction between them, a possibility of separation and alliance.

[4] *The Philosophical Works of Descartes*, trans. E. S. Haldane and G. R. T. Ross, (Cambridge: Cambridge University Press, 1931; reprinted Dover, 1955), 1: 358.

This might take place at the time of the first meeting, even prior to the betrothal, and remain as a permanent proof of difference. The *interval* would never be *crossed*. Consummation would never take place, the idea itself being a delusion. One sex is not entirely consumable by the other. There is always a *remainder*.

Up until now this remainder has been entrusted to or reserved for *God*. Sometimes a portion was incarnated in the *child*. Or was thought of as being *neuter*. This neuter (in a different way, like the child or God?) suggests the possibility of an encounter but puts it off, deferring it until later, even when it is a question of a secondary revision [*après-coup*]. It always stays at an insurmountable distance, a respectful or deadly sort of no-man's-land:[5] no alliance is forged; nothing is celebrated. The immediacy of the encounter is annihilated or deferred to a future that never comes.

Of course, the neuter might signify an alchemical site of the sublimation of "genitality," and the possibility of generation, of the creation of and between different genders and genres. But it would still have to be receptive to the advent of difference, and be understood as an anticipation from this side and not as a beyond, especially an ethical one. Generally the phrase *there is* upholds the present but defers celebration. There is not, there will not be the moment of wonder of the *wedding*, an ecstasy that remains *in-stant*.[6] The *there is* remains a present that may be subject to pressure by the god, but it does not form a foundation for the triumph of sexual fecundity. Only certain oriental traditions speak of the energizing, aesthetic, and religious fecundity of the sexual act: the two sexes give each other the seed of life and eternity, the growing generation of and between them both.

We must reexamine our own history thoroughly to under-

---

[5] (In English in the original text.—Tr.)

[6] (*Instance* is rendered here as "in-stant" to underscore Irigaray's emphasis on the term's root meaning, standing within the self, as opposed to "ecstasy," standing outside the self.—Tr.)

stand why this sexual difference has not had its chance to develop, either empirically or transcendentally. Why it has failed to have its own ethics, aesthetic, logic, religion, or the micro- and macrocosmic realization of its coming into being or its destiny.

It is surely a question of the dissociation of body and soul, of sexuality and spirituality, of the lack of a passage for the spirit, for the god, between the inside and the outside, the outside and the inside, and of their distribution between the sexes in the sexual act. Everything is constructed in such a way that these realities remain separate, even opposed to one another. So that they neither mix, marry, nor form an alliance. Their wedding is always being put off to a beyond, a future life, or else devalued, felt and thought to be less worthy in comparison to the marriage between the mind and God in a transcendental realm where all ties to the world of sensation have been severed.

The consequences of the nonfulfillment of the sexual act remain, and there are many. To take up only the most beautiful, as yet to be made manifest in the realm of time and space, there are *angels*. These messengers who never remain enclosed in a place, who are also never immobile. Between God, as the perfectly immobile act, man, who is surrounded and enclosed by the world of his work, and woman, whose task would be to take care of nature and procreation, *angels* would circulate as mediators of that which has not yet happened, of what is still going to happen, of what is on the horizon. Endlessly reopening the enclosure of the universe, of universes, identities, the unfolding of actions, of history.

The angel is that which unceasingly *passes through the envelope(s)* or *container(s)*, goes from one side to the other, reworking every deadline, changing every decision, thwarting all repetition. Angels destroy the monstrous, that which hampers the possibility of a new age; they come to herald the arrival of a new birth, a new morning.

They are not unrelated to sex. There is of course Gabriel, the

[15]

angel of the annunciation. But other angels announce the consummation of marriage, notably all the angels in the Apocalypse
and many in the Old Testament. As if the angel were a representation of a sexuality that has never been incarnated. A light,
divine gesture (or tale) of flesh that has not yet acted or flour-
ished. Always fallen or still awaiting parousia. The fate of a love
still torn between here and elsewhere. The work of a love that is
the original sinner, since the first garden, the lost earthly paradise? The fate of all flesh which is, moreover, attributable to
God![7]

These swift angelic messengers, who transgress all enclosures
in their speed, tell of the passage between the envelope of God
and that of the world as micro- or macrocosm. They proclaim
that such a journey can be made by the body of man, and above
all the body of woman. They represent and tell of another incarnation, another parousia of the body. Irreducible to philosophy,
theology, morality, angels appear as the messengers of ethics
evoked by art—sculpture, painting, or music—without its being possible to say anything more than the gesture that represents them.

They speak like messengers, but gesture seems to be their
"nature." Movement, posture, the coming-and-going between
the two. They move—or stir up?—the paralysis or *apatheia* of
the body, or the soul, or the world. They set trances or convul-
sions to music, or give them harmony.

Their touch—when they touch—resembles that of gods.
They are imperious in their grace even as they remain imperceptible.

One of the questions which arises about them is whether they
can be found together in the same place. The traditional answer
is no. This question, which is similar to and different from that
of the co-location of bodies, comes back to the question of

[7] See Luce Irigaray, "Epistle to the Last Christians," in *Marine Lover of Friedrich
Nietzsche*, trans. Gillian C. Gill (New York: Columbia University Press, 1991).

sexual ethics. The mucous should no doubt be pictured as related to the angel, whereas the inertia of the body deprived of its relation to the mucous and its gesture is linked to the fallen body or the corpse.

A sexual or carnal ethics would require that both angel and body be found together. This is a world that must be constructed or reconstructed. A genesis of love between the sexes has yet to come about in all dimensions, from the smallest to the greatest, from the most intimate to the most political. A world that must be created or re-created so that man and woman may once again or at last live together, meet, and sometimes inhabit the same place.

The link uniting or reuniting masculine and feminine must be horizontal and vertical, terrestrial and heavenly. As Heidegger, among others, has written, it must forge an alliance between the divine and the mortal, such that the sexual encounter would be a festive celebration and not a disguised or polemical form of the master-slave relationship. Nor a meeting in the shadow or orbit of a Father-God who alone lays down the law, who is the immutable spokesman of a single sex.

Of course, the most extreme progression and regression goes under the name of God. I can only strive toward the absolute or regress to infinity under the guarantee of God's existence. This is what tradition has taught us, and its imperatives have not yet been overcome, since their destruction brings about terrible abandonments and pathological states, unless one has exceptional love partners. And even then . . . Unhappiness is sometimes all the more inescapable when it lacks the horizon of the divine, of the gods, of an opening onto a beyond, but also a *limit* that the other may or may not penetrate.

How can we mark this limit of a place, of place in general, if not through sexual difference? But, in order for an ethics of sexual difference to come into being, we must constitute a possible place for each sex, body, and flesh to inhabit. Which presupposes a memory of the past, a hope for the future, memory bridging the present and disconcerting the mirror symmetry that annihilates the difference of identity.

To do this requires time, both space and time. Perhaps we are passing through an era when *time must redeploy space*? A new morning of and for the world? A remaking of immanence and transcendence, notably through this *threshold* which has never been examined as such: the female sex. The threshold that gives access to the *mucous*. Beyond classical oppositions of love and hate, liquid and ice—a threshold that is always *half-open*. The threshold of the *lips*, which are strangers to dichotomy and oppositions. Gathered one against the other but without any possible suture, at least of a real kind. They do not absorb the world into or through themselves, provided they are not misused and reduced to a means of consumption or consummation. They offer a shape of welcome but do not assimilate, reduce, or swallow up. A sort of doorway to voluptuousness? They are not useful, except as that which designates a *place*, the very place of uselessness, at least as it is habitually understood. Strictly speaking, they serve neither conception nor jouissance. Is this the mystery of feminine identity? Of its self-contemplation, of this very strange word of silence? Both the threshold and reception of exchange, the sealed-up secret of wisdom, belief, and faith in all truths?

(Two sets of lips that, moreover, cross over each other like the arms of the cross, the prototype of the crossroads *between*. The mouth lips and the genital lips do not point in the same direction. In some way they point in the direction opposite from the one you would expect, with the "lower" ones forming the vertical.)

In this approach, where the borders of the body are wed in an embrace that transcends all limits—without, however, risking engulfment, thanks to the fecundity of the porous—in the most extreme experience of sensation, which is also always in the future, each one discovers the self in that experience which is inexpressible yet forms the supple grounding of life and language.

For this, "God" is necessary, or a love so attentive that it is divine. Which has never taken place? Love always postpones its transcendence beyond the here and now, except in certain experiences of God. And desire fails to act sufficiently on the porous nature of the body, omitting the communion that takes place through the most intimate mucous membranes. In this exchange, what is communicated is so subtle that one needs great perseverance to keep it from falling into oblivion, intermittency, deterioration, illness, or death.

This communion is often left to the child, as the symbol of the union. But there are other signs of union which precede the child—the space where the lovers give each other life or death? Regeneration or degeneration: both are possible. The intensity of desire and the filiation of both lovers are engaged.

And if the divine is present as the mystery that animates the copula, the *is* and the *being* in sexual difference, can the force of desire overcome the avatars of genealogical destiny? How does it manage this? With what power [*puissance*] does it reckon, while remaining nevertheless incarnate? Between the idealistic fluidity of an unborn body that is untrue to its birth and genetic determinism, how do we take the measure of a love that changes our condition from mortal to immortal? Certain figures of gods become men, of God become man, and of twice-born beings indicate the path of love.

Has something of the achievement of sexual difference still not been said or transmitted? Has something been held in reserve within the silence of a history in the feminine: an energy, a morphology, a growth and flourishing still to come from the female realm? An overture to a future that is still and always open? Given that the world has remained aporetic about this strange advent.

[*19*]

Sorcerer Love:

A Reading of Plato,

Symposium, "Diotima's Speech"

In the *Symposium*, the dialogue on love, when Socrates finishes speaking, he gives the floor to a woman: Diotima. She does not take part in these exchanges or in this meal among men. She is not there. She herself does not speak. Socrates reports or recounts her words. He praises her for her wisdom and her power and declares that she is his initiator or teacher when it comes to love, but she is not invited to teach or to eat. Unless she didn't want to accept an invitation? But Socrates says nothing about that. And Diotima is not the only example of a woman whose wisdom, especially about love, is reported in her absence by a man.

Diotima's teaching will be very dialectical, but different from what we usually call dialectical. In effect, it doesn't use opposition to make the first term pass into the second in order to achieve a synthesis of the two, as Hegel does. From the outset, she establishes an *intermediary* that will never be abandoned as a means or a path. Her method, then, is not a propaedeutic of the *destruction* or the *destructuration* of two terms in order to establish a synthesis that is neither one nor the other. She presents, uncovers, unveils the insistence of a third term that is already there and that permits progression: from poverty to wealth, from ignorance to wisdom, from mortality to immortality. Which, for her, always comes to a greater perfection of and in love.

But, contrary to the usual methods of dialectic, one should not have to give up love in order to become wise or learned. It is love that leads to knowledge, whether in art or more metaphysical learning. It is love that both leads the way and is the path. A mediator par excellence.

This mediating role is indicated as part of the theme, but it is also perpetually at issue, on stage, in the exposition of the theme.

Thus, Diotima immediately refutes the claim that love, Eros, is a great God[1] and that it is the love of beautiful things. At the risk of offending the practice of respect for the Gods, she also asserts that Eros is neither beautiful nor good. This leads her interlocutor to suppose immediately that Eros is ugly and bad, as he is incapable of grasping the existence or the in-stance of that which stands *between*, that which makes possible the passage between ignorance and knowledge. If we did not, at each moment, have something to learn from the encounter with reality, between reality and already established knowledge, we would not perfect ourselves in wisdom. And not to become wiser means to become more ignorant.

Therefore, between knowledge and reality, there is an intermediary that allows for the encounter and the transmutation or transvaluation between the two. Diotima's dialectic is in at least *four terms*: the here, the two poles of the encounter, and the beyond—but a beyond that never abolishes the here. And so on, indefinitely. The mediator is never abolished in an infallible knowledge. Everything is always in movement, in a state of becoming. And the mediator of all this is, among other things, or exemplarily, *love*. Never fulfilled, always becoming.

[1] (Capitalization of words in the English translation follows the usage in the original French text.—Tr.)

And, in response to Socrates' protestation that love is a great God, that *everyone says so or thinks so*, she *laughs*. Her retort is not at all angry, the effect of hesitating between contradictory positions; it is laughter based on other grounds. While laughing, then, she asks Socrates what he means by *everyone*. Just as she ceaselessly dismantles the assurance or *closure* of opposing terms, she undoes all *sets* of units reduced to sameness in order to constitute a whole. "'*You mean, by all who do not know?' said she, 'or by all who know as well?'—'Absolutely all.' At that she laughed.*" (Plato, *Symposium* 202; p. 252).[2] Once the tension between opposites has subsided in this way, she shows, or demonstrates, that "everyone" does not exist, nor does love's position as *always* a great God. Does she teach nothing that is already defined? A method of becoming wise, learned, more perfected in love and in art. Thus she ceaselessly examines Socrates on his positions but without positing authoritative, already constituted truths. Instead, she teaches the renunciation of already established truths. And each time Socrates thinks he can take something as certain, she undoes his certainty. His own, but also all kinds of certainty that are already set in language. All entities, substantives, adverbs, sentences are patiently, and joyously, called into question.

For love, or Eros, the demonstration is not so difficult to establish. For if Eros possessed all that he desired, he would desire no more. He must be lacking in order to desire still. But if he had no share in the beautiful and the good things, he could no longer desire them. He is therefore an *intermediary* in a very specific way. Does he lose his status as a God for this reason? Not necessarily. He is neither mortal nor immortal. He is between the one and the other, in a state that can be qualified as

---

[2] Page references following the quotations from Plato are to Lane Cooper's translation of the *Symposium* in his *Phaedrus, Ion, Gorgias, and Symposium, with passages from the Republic and Laws* (London: Oxford University Press, 1938).

daimonic: love is a *daimon*.[3] His function is to transmit to the gods what comes from men and to men what comes from the gods. Like all that is daimonic, love is complementary to gods and to men in such a way as to put everything in touch with itself. A being of middle nature is needed so that men and gods can enter into relations, into conversation, while awake or asleep. This need is expressed in divination, in the priestly knowledge of things related to sacrifices, initiations, incantations, preaching in general, and magic.

Daimons serving as mediators between men and gods are numerous and very diverse. Eros is one of them. And his parentage is exceptional: he is the child of *Plenty* (who is the son of *Invention*) and of *Poverty*, and he was conceived on the day when the birth of Aphrodite was celebrated. So, Diotima tells Socrates, Eros is always poor and "*rough, unkempt, unshod, and homeless, ever couching on the ground uncovered, sleeping beneath the open sky by doors and in the streets, because he has the nature of his mother. . . . But again, in keeping with his father, he has designs upon the beautiful and good, for he is bold, headlong, and intense, a mighty hunter, always weaving some device or other, eager in invention and resourceful, searching after wisdom all through life, terrible as a magician, sorcerer, and sophist.*

"*As for ignorance and knowledge, here again he is midway between them. The case stands thus. No god seeks after wisdom, or wishes to grow wise (for he already is so), any more than anybody else seeks after wisdom if he has it. Nor, again, do ignorant folk seek after wisdom or long to grow wise; for here is just the trouble about ignorance, that what is neither beautiful and good, nor yet intelligent, to itself seems good enough. Accordingly, the man who does not think himself in need has no desire for what he does not think himself in need of.*"

Socrates protests: "*The seekers after knowledge, Diotima! If they are not the wise, nor yet the ignorant, who are they, then?*"

---

[3] (*Démon* is translated here as "daimon," from the Greek for a tutelary divinity, a spirit. —Tr.)

"The point," said she, *"is obvious even to a child, that they are persons intermediate between these two, and that Eros is among them; for wisdom falls within the class of the most beautiful, while Eros is an eros for the beautiful. And hence it follows necessarily that Eros is a seeker after wisdom [a philosopher], and being a philosopher, is midway between wise and ignorant."* (203–4; pp. 253–54).

Love is thus an intermediary *between* pairs of opposites: poverty/plenty, ignorance/wisdom, ugliness/beauty, dirtiness/cleanliness, death/life, and so on. And this would be inscribed in his nature given his genealogy and the date of his conception. And love is a philosopher and a philosophy. Philosophy is not a formal learning, fixed and rigid, abstracted from all feeling. It is a quest for love, love of beauty, love of wisdom, which is one of the most beautiful things. Like love, the philosopher would be someone poor, dirty, rather down-and-out, always unhoused, sleeping beneath the stars, but very curious, skilled in ruses and tricks of all kinds, constantly reflecting, a sorcerer, a sophist, sometimes exuberant, sometimes close to death. This is nothing like the way we usually represent the philosopher: a learned person who is well dressed, has good manners, knows everything, and pedantically instructs us in the corpus of things already coded. The philosopher is nothing like that. He is a sort of barefoot waif who goes out under the stars seeking an encounter with reality, the embrace, the knowledge or perhaps a shared birth [*connaissance, co-naissance*], of whatever benevolence, beauty, or wisdom might be found there. He inherits this endless quest from his mother. He is a philosopher through his mother and skilled in art through his father. But his passion for love, for beauty, for wisdom comes to him from his mother, and from the date that he was conceived. Desired and wanted, moreover, by his mother.

How does it happen that love and the philosopher are generally represented otherwise? Because they are imagined as *beloveds* and not as *lovers*. As a beloved, Love, both like and unlike the philosopher, is imagined to be of unparalleled beauty, delicate, perfect, and happy. Yet the lover is of an entirely different nature. He goes toward what is kind, beautiful, perfect, and so on. He doesn't possess it. He is poor, unhappy, always in search of. . . . But what does he seek or love? That beautiful things become his—this is Socrates' reply. But what happens to him if these things become his? To this question interjected by Diotima, Socrates cannot respond. Substituting "good" for "beautiful," she repeats the question. *"That the good may be his,"* repeats Socrates. *"And what happens to the man when the good things become his?"* *"On this,"* said Socrates, *"I am more than ready with an answer: that he will be happy"* (204–5; pp. 254–55). And happiness seems to put an ultimate term to this dialogical volleying between Diotima and Socrates.

How should we name that which is fitting to lovers? "By what manner of pursuit and in what activity does the eagerness and straining for the object get the name of Eros? And what may this action really be?" asks Socrates. And Diotima answers: *"This action is engendering in beauty, with relation both to body and to soul"* (206; p. 256). But Socrates understands nothing of such a clear revelation. He understands nothing about fecundity of body and soul. *"The union of a man and woman is, in fact, a generation; this is a thing divine; in a living creature that is mortal, it is an element of immortality, this fecundity and generation"* (206; p. 256). This statement of Diotima's never seems to have been heard. Moreover, she herself goes on to accentuate the procreative aspect of love. But first she emphasizes the character of *divine generation in any union between man and woman*, the presence of immortality in the living mortal. All love is seen as creation and potentially divine, a path between the condition of the mortal and that of the immortal. Love is fecund prior to any procreation. And its fecundity is *mediumlike, daimonic,* the guarantee for all, male and female, of the immortal becoming of the living. But there cannot be procreation of a divine nature where harmony is lacking. And the divine cannot be in harmony with the ugly, only with the beautiful. So, according to Diotima, love between man and woman is beautiful, harmonious, divine. It must be so for procreation to take place. It is not procreation that is beautiful and that constitutes the objective of love. Love's aim is to realize the immortal in the mortal between lovers. And the energy pouring forth to produce the child results from joy at the approach of a beautiful object. Whereas an unattractive object results in a withdrawal, a hoarding of fecundity, the painfully borne weight of the desire to procreate. Procreation and generation in beauty—this is the aim of love. Because in this way the eternity and the imperishability of a mortal being are made manifest.

Fecundity of love between lovers—the regeneration of one by the other, the passage to immortality in and through each other—this seems to become the condition of procreation and not a cause in its own right. Of course, Diotima says to Socrates that the creation of beauty, of a work of art (by oneself this time?) does not suffice, that it is necessary to create a child together, that this wisdom is inscribed in the animal world itself. She continues to laugh at his going to look for his truths beyond the most obvious everyday reality, at his not seeing or even perceiving this reality. At the way in which his dialectical or dialogical method already forgets the most elementary truths. At the way his discourse on love neglects to look at, to be informed, about the amorous state. Or to inquire about its cause.

Diotima speaks of *cause* in an astonishing way. One could expect that her method would not enter into the chain of causalities, a chain that skips over or often forgets about the intermediary as a generative middle term. Causality doesn't usually play a part in her progression. She borrows it from the animal world and evokes or invokes it on the subject of procreation. Instead of leaving the child to germinate or ripen in the milieu of love and fecundity between man and woman, she seeks a cause for love in the animal world: *procreation*. Diotima's method miscarries here. From this point on, she leads love into a split between mortality and immortality, and love loses its daimonic character. Is this the foundational act of meta-physics? There will be lovers in body, lovers in soul. But the perpetual passage from mortal to immortal that lovers confer on each other is blurred. Love has lost its divinity, its mediumistic, alchemical qualities between couples of opposites. Since love is no longer the intermediary, the child plays this role. Occupying the space of love, the child can no longer be a lover and is put in the place of love's incessant movement. It is beloved, no doubt. But how can one be loved without being a lover? And isn't love trapped there *in the beloved*, contrary to what Diotima wanted in the first place? A beloved who is an *end* is substituted for love between men and women. A beloved who is a *will*, even a *duty*, and a *means* of attaining immortality, which the lovers can neither attain nor aspire to between themselves. This is the failure of love, for the child as well. If the pair of lovers cannot safeguard the place for love as a third term between them, they can neither remain lovers nor give birth to lovers. Something becomes frozen in space-time, with the loss of a vital intermediary and of an accessible transcendental that remains alive. A sort of teleological triangle is put into place instead of a perpetual journey, a perpetual transvaluation, a permanent becoming. For this, love was the vehicle. But, if procreation becomes its goal, it risks losing its internal motivation, its "inner" fecundity, its slow and constant generation, regeneration. This error in method, in the originality of Diotima's method, is corrected soon afterward only to be confirmed later. Of course, once again, *she is not there. Socrates relates her words.* Perhaps he distorts them unwittingly or unknowingly.

The following paragraph, moreover, goes against what was

just asserted. It tells how a permanent renewal takes place in us. How there is in us an unending loss of what is old or already dead, both at the most physical level—hair, bones, blood, our whole body—and in our spiritual aspect—our character, our opinions, our desires, joys and pains, our fears. None of these elements is ever the same as what it was for us, in that some come into existence while others perish. And the same is true for knowledge that is acquired and forgotten—thus in constant renewal. It is in this fashion *"in which everything mortal is preserved, not in being always perfectly identical, as is divinity, but in that the disappearing and decaying object leaves behind it another new one such as it was. By this arrangement, Socrates,"* said she, *"the mortal partakes of immortality, both in body and all else; the immortal does so in another way. So do not marvel if everything by nature prizes its own offspring; it is for the sake of immortality that every being has this urgency and love"* (208; p. 258). Here, Diotima returns to her type of argumentation, including her mockery of those who suspend the present in order to search "for endless time, imperishable glory" (208; p. 259). She speaks—and notably through her style, which *entwines with* what she says without *tying the knot*— of becoming in time, of the permanent generation-regeneration that takes place here and now in everyone, male and female, as far as corporeal and spiritual realities are concerned. Without going so far as to say that the one is the fruition of the other. Rather, that at each moment, we are a "regrowth" of ourselves, in perpetual increase. No more searching for immortality through the child. But in ourselves, ceaselessly. Diotima returns to a progression that admits love as it had been defined before she evoked procreation: as an intermediate terrain, a mediator, a space-time of permanent *passage* between mortal and immortal.

Then, returning to an example of the quest for immortality through fame, she resituates the object (of) love outside of the subject: in renown, immortal glory, and so on. No more of constantly becoming immortal in ourselves but instead a race toward something that would confer immortality. Similarly and differently as for the procreation of a child, the stake of love is placed outside the self. In the beloved and not in the lover? The lovers mentioned, Alcestis, Admetus, Achilles, Codrus, were cited only so that we would always remember them. It was with the goal of immortal fame that they loved until death. Immortality is the object of their love. Not love itself. *"Well then,"* Diotima said, *"when men's fecundity is of the body, they turn rather to the women, and the fashion of their love is this: through begetting children to provide themselves with immortality, renown and happiness, as they imagine, securing them for all time to come.*

"But when fecundity is of the soul—for indeed there are those persons who are fecund in their souls even more than in their bodies, fecund in what is the function of the soul to conceive and also to bring forth— what is this proper offspring? It is wisdom, along with every other spiritual value" (208–9; p. 259). What seemed to me to be original in Diotima's method has disappeared once again. This intermediary milieu of love, which is irreducible, is resplit between a "subject" (an inadequate word in Plato) and a "beloved reality." Falling in love no longer constitutes a becoming of the lover himself, of love in the lover (male or female), or between the lovers, but is now the teleological quest for what is deemed a higher reality and often situated in a transcendence inaccessible to our mortal condition. Immortality has already been put off until death and does not figure as one of our constant tasks as mortals, a transmutation that is endlessly incumbent upon us here, now—its possibility having been inscribed in the body, which is capable of becoming divine. Beauty of body and of soul are hierarchized, and the love of women becomes the lot of those who, incapable of being creators in soul, are fecund of body and expect the immortality of their name to be perpetuated through their offspring.

"By far the greatest and most beautiful form of wisdom," said she, *"is that which has to do with regulating states and households, and has the name, no doubt, of 'temperance' and 'justice'."* (209; p. 259).

To fall in love, to become divine, or immortal, is no longer left to the intermediary current but qualified, hierarchized. And in the worst case, love dies as a result. In the universe of determinations, there will be goals, competitions, and loving duties, the beloved or love being the goal. The lovers disappear. Our subsequent tradition has even taught us that it is forbidden or futile to be lovers unless there is procreation, whereas Diotima had begun by affirming that the most divine act is "the union of man and woman, a divine affair." What she asserted at that moment accorded with what she said about the function of love as an intermediary that remains an intermediary, a daimon. It seems that during the course of her speech, she diminishes somewhat this daimonic, mediumistic function of love, such that it is no longer really a daimon, but an intention, a reduction to the intention, to the teleology of human will, already subjected to a kind of thought with fixed objectives, not an immanent efflorescence of the divine of and in the flesh. Love was meant to be an irreducible mediator, at once physical and spiritual, between the lovers, and not already codified duty, will, desire. Love that is still invoked as a daimon in a method aiming toward the beautiful and the good often disappears from discourse, reappearing only in art, "painting," in the form(s) of cupids that excite eroticism, and, perhaps, in the form of angels. Is love itself split between *eros* and *agape*? Yet, for lovers to love each other, between them there must be Love.

There remains what was said about love, the philosopher. But why wouldn't philosopher-Love be a lover of the other? A lover only of the Other? Or of an inaccessible transcendent. In any case, such would already be the ideal whenever daimonic love is suppressed. Love becomes political wisdom, the wisdom of order in the city, not the intermediary state that inhabits lovers and transports them from the condition of mortals to that of immortals. Love becomes a kind of *raison d'état*. It founds a family, takes care of children, and of all those children who are the citizens. The more its objective is distanced from individual becoming, the more valuable it is. Its stake gets lost in the immortal good and beautiful seen as collective goods. The family is preferable to the generating of lovers, between lovers. Adopted children are preferable to others. It is in this way, moreover, that it comes to pass that *love between men is superior to love between man and woman*. Carnal procreation is subordinated to the engendering of beautiful and good things. Immortal things. This, surprisingly enough, is the view of Diotima. At least as translated through the words of Socrates.

The beings most gifted in wisdom go directly to this end. Most begin by going toward physical beauty and *"must love one single object [physical form of beauty], and thereof must engender fair discourses"* (210; p. 260). If the instruction is properly done, this must be so. But whoever becomes attached to one body must learn that beauty resides in many. After having pursued beauty in one perceptible form, he must learn that the same beauty resides in all bodies; he will *"abate his violent love of one, disdaining this and deeming it a trifle, and will become a lover of all fair objects"* (210; p. 261). From the attraction to a single beautiful body, he passes then to many; and from there to the beauty residing in souls. Thus he learns that beauty is not housed only in the body and that someone of an unattractive bodily appearance can be beautiful and kind; that to be just is to know how to take care of him and to engender beautiful discourse for him. Thus love passes imperceptibly into love of works. The passion for beautiful bodies is transmuted into the discovery of the beauty found in knowledge. That which liberates from the attachment to a single master opens to the immense ocean of the beautiful and leads to the birth of numerous and sublime discourses, as well as thoughts inspired by a boundless love of wisdom. Until the point when the force and the development that he will have found there allow him to perceive *one single* knowledge (210; p. 261). This marvelous beauty is perceptible, perhaps, by whoever has been led along the path just described, by whoever has passed step-by-step through the different stages. He will then have the vision of a beauty *"which is eternal, not growing up or perishing, increasing or decreasing*" and which is moreover *absolutely* beautiful, "*not beautiful in one point and ugly in another, nor sometimes beautiful and sometimes not; not beautiful in one relation and ugly in another, nor beautiful in this place and ugly in that, as if beautiful to some, to others ugly; again, this beauty will not be revealed to him in the semblance of a face, or hands, or any other element of the body, nor in any form of speech or knowledge, nor yet as if it appertained to any other being, a creature, for example, upon earth, or in the sky, or elsewhere; no, it will be seen as beauty in and for itself, consistent with itself in uniformity forever, whereas all other beauties share it in such fashion that, while they are ever born and perish, that eternal beauty, never waxing, never waning, never is impaired.*" (211; pp. 261–62).

To attain this sublime beauty, one must begin with the love of young men. Starting with their natural beauty, one must, step-by-step, ascend to supernatural beauty: from beautiful bodies pass to beautiful occupations, then to beautiful sciences, until one reaches that sublime science which is supernatural beauty alone, which allows the isolated knowledge of the essence of beauty (211; p. 262). This contemplation is what gives the meaning and savor of life: "*It will not appear to you to be according to the measure of gold and raiment, or of lovely boys and striplings.*" (211; p. 262). And what can he who has perceived "*beauty in its own single nature*" ever look at again? Having contemplated "*the beautiful with that by which it can be seen*" (212; p. 262), beyond all simulacra, he is united with it and *truly* virtuous; since he attained "authentic reality," he becomes dear to the divine and is made immortal.

This person would have then attained what I shall call a *sensible transcendental*, the material texture of beauty. He would have "seen" the very spatiality of the visible, the real which precedes all reality, all forms, all truth of particular sensations or constructed idealities. He would have contemplated the "nature" of the divine? This support of the fabrication of the transcendent in its different modes, all of which, according to Diotima, come under the same propaedeutic: *love of beauty*. Neither the good nor the true nor justice nor government of the city would occur without beauty. And its best ally is love. Love therefore deserves veneration. And Diotima asks that her words be considered as a celebration and praise of Love.

In the second part of her discourse, she treated Love itself as a means. She doubled its intermediary function and subjected it to a *telos*. Her method seems less powerful here than at the beginning of her remarks, when she held love to be the mediator of a state of becoming with no objective other than becoming. Perhaps Diotima is still saying the same thing. But in the second part, her method runs the risk of being reduced to the metaphysics that is getting set up. Unless what she proposes to contemplate, beauty itself, is seen as that which confounds the opposition between immanence and transcendence. As an always already sensible horizon on the basis of which everything would appear. But one would have to go back over everything to discover it in its enchantment.

Place, Interval:
A Reading of Aristotle,
Physics IV

"*Further, too, if it is itself an existent, it will be somewhere. Zeno's difficulty demands an explanation: for if everything that exists has a place, place too will have a place, and so on* ad infinitum." (Aristotle, *Physics* IV, 209a, fifth difficulty; p. 355).[1]

If the matrix is extendable, it can figure as *the place of place*. It is the first place that can ever be situated in a progression to infinity. So, does this explain the nostalgia? The entry into an indefinite number of places? The quest for the unique in the downshift of places? The belief in a certain God so as to stop falling or expanding immediately to infinity through the suppression of all platforms of duration, of space-time.

I go on a quest through an indefinite number of bodies, through nature, through God, for the body that once served as place for me, where I (male/female) was able to stay contained, enveloped.[2] Given that, as far as man is concerned, the issue is to separate the first and the last place. Which can lead to a double

[1] Page references following the quotations from Aristotle, *Physics* IV, 1–5, are to *The Complete Works of Aristotle: The Revised Oxford Translation*, ed. Jonathan Barnes, trans. R. P. Hardie and R. K. Gaye (Oxford: Oxford University Press, 1987), 1:354–62.

[2] (The French translations of Aristotle cited by Irigaray use different forms of the word "envelope," whereas the English translations refer to "container." Since "envelope" has been an important word in Irigaray's vocabulary since *Speculum of the Other Woman*, this translation frequently doubles "container"

downshift: both of the relation to the unique mother and of the relation to the unique God. Can these two downshifts come together? Can the quest to infinity for the mother in women result in a quest for infinity in God? Or do the two quests intersect ceaselessly? With place indefinitely switching from the one to the other? Modifying itself moment by moment. Or even transmuting itself from one envelope to the other? I become for God the container, the envelope, the vessel, the place for which I quest? Nonetheless the split between first and last place has still to be resolved.

As for woman, she is place. Does she have to locate herself in bigger and bigger places? But also to find, situate, in herself, the place that she is. If she is unable to constitute, within herself, the place that she is, she passes ceaselessly through the child in order to return to herself. She turns around an object in order to return to herself. And this captures the other in her interiority. For this not to occur, she has to assume the passage between *the infinitely large* and *the infinitely small*. Given that, ultimately, those two places cannot really be delineated. Except perhaps as *a grain of sand* in the reasoning of man? Or as *nest in her for her*? Passage from one place to another, for her, remains the problem of place as such, always within the context of the mobility of her constitution. She is able to move within place as place. Within the availability of place. Given that her issue is how to trace the limits of place herself so as to be able to situate herself therein and welcome the other there. If she is to be able to contain, to envelop, she must have her own envelope. Not only her clothing and ornaments of seduction, but her skin. And her skin must contain a receptacle. She must lack
— neither body,
— nor extension within,
— nor extension without,
or she will plummet down and take the other with her.

and "envelope" in order to link the text both with the cited passages from Aristotle and with Irigaray's earlier writings.—Tr.)

And this fall continues to infinity, since there is nothing to stop it:
  — given that returning to the mother is impracticable, or impossible,
  — given the world here below, life and death itself in relation to God,
  — given that sexual difference is irreducible.

"*Again, just as every body is in place, so, too, every place has a body in it. What then shall we say about* growing *things? It follows from these premises that their place must grow with them, if their place is neither less nor greater than they are.*" (209a, 6th difficulty, p. 355).
  Another difficulty reinforces those of
  — life in the womb,
  — sexual relation,
or indeed the difficulties posed by nature and by place and body in their as yet uncovered principial relations, both physical and metaphysical.
  At issue is the extension of place, of places, and of the relation of that extension to the development of the body and bodies. An issue either forgotten or ignored in the junction of physics and metaphysics, since these two dimensions have been set aside or dislocated, but an issue still alive today (resurrected from its place of repression, psychoanalysts might say).

  In this journeying from one place to another, one must distinguish "*place which is common and in which all bodies are*" from that "*which is the proper and primary location of each body.*" (209a, 2; p. 356).
  The universe contains all bodies. The sky, the air, the earth are containers that are not specific to each of us (male or female). But each of us (male or female) has a place—this place that envelops only his or her body, the first envelope of our bodies, the corporeal identity, the boundary, that which delineates us from other bodies. Form and configuration also determine one's

size and all that makes one body unsubstitutable by another. Could this be called a corporeal *surveying*? As well as a virtual one. For this place is the form of each thing but also its extendable matter or the interval of size. It is—according to Plato, with whom Aristotle agrees on this issue—both *container* and *extension*. Which means that it must also be growth between the different forms. And that growth is not alien to it. That growth is in some way given within and with place itself. Yet, since place participates in the determinations of matter and form, it is hard to penetrate. Separated one from the other, matter and form are similarly difficult to penetrate.

Place would in some way be the "nature" of matter and form, the habitat in which both wed without ceasing, and in their extension. To infinity.

This would be so for both masculine and feminine if the split between them (in the division of both work and nature) were bridged. But it can be bridged only by passing back through the definition of place and of the singular situation of the sexes in relation to place.

"*But it is at any rate not difficult to see that place cannot be either of them. The form and the matter are not separate from the thing, whereas the place can be separated. As we pointed out, where air was, water in turn comes to be, the one replacing the other; and similarly with other bodies. Hence the place of a thing is neither a part nor a state of it, but separable from it. For place is supposed to be something like a vessel— the vessel being a transportable place. But the vessel is no part of the thing. In so far, then, as it is separable from the thing, it is not the form: qua containing, it is different from the matter.*" (209b, first reason; p. 356).

Place cannot be simply matter *or* form, on one side or the other side of growth and becoming. Thus, matter *and* form cannot be separated from the thing; place can. In fact place reveals itself as a result of that separability. Without being reduced to either a part or a state of either matter or form, it appears like a *vessel* (which may possibly be a variant of place because it is subject to *locomotion?*).

This means:

— it is not to be reduced to form in that it is separable from the thing,

— it is not to be reduced to matter in that it is a container or envelope.

Is it defined here as a mold that embraces the thing? Or else receives it? A transportable mold. Neither coextensive with nature nor adhering to it, since it can be moved.

"*Also it is held that what is anywhere is both itself something and that there is a different thing outside it.*" (209b, second reason; p. 257).

That this bond is neither matter nor form is also evident from the fact that anything that is situated somewhere is per se some thing; given that only through its situation is this thing in a "thing" other than itself. Place is thus not the thing but that which permits the thing to be insofar as the thing can exist in and outside place.

"(*Plato, of course, if we may digress, ought to tell us why the form*[3] *and the numbers are not in place, if 'what participates' is place— whether what participates is the Great and the Small or the matter, as he has written in the Timaeus.*)" (209b, third reason; p. 357).

What is the nature of ideas and numbers if they are not part of place even though place has its role to play in the great and the small? This question, which Aristotle treats as a digression, is in fact essential. Where are ideas and numbers situated if they are not in place? Even though they must borrow "matter" from place if they are to exist? Do ideas and numbers bring place down on the side of residual matter? Or the empirical? Does

---

[3] (In the French Budé edition used by Irigaray, this phrase is rendered as "les idées et les nombres."—Tr.)

[*38*]

their nonsituation in place consecrate a split between sensible and ideal? Leaving undecided the issue of where ideas and numbers come from? As well, perhaps, as the issue of their inscription in the world? Is this duality of place, on the one hand, and ideas and numbers, on the other, one of the symptoms of the divorce between masculine and feminine? In order to overcome the attraction for the first and unique place, does man, at his best, practice with ideas and numbers as independent from place? This "ascension," which is not inscribed in place, makes a return to place possible only in the form of a downfall, a plunging into the abyss, and so on.

"Further, how could a body be carried to its own place, if place was the matter or the form? It is impossible that what has no reference to motion or the distinction of up and down can be place. So place must be looked for among those things which have these characteristics." (210a, fourth reason; p. 357).

The independence of place in relation to matter and form may be understood by this to mean that place itself is that toward which there is *locomotion*. When separated from place, the thing feels an attraction to place as a condition of existence. If I may return to the parallel I have been drawing between the issue of place and the issue of sexual difference, I shall affirm that the masculine is attracted to the maternal-feminine as place. But what place does the masculine offer to attract the feminine? His soul? His relation to the divine? Can the feminine be inscribed or situated there? Is this not the only place where he can live, contrary to what has always been assumed? For the masculine has to constitute itself as a *vessel* to receive and welcome. And the masculine's morphology, existence, and essence do not really fit it for such an architecture of place. Except through a reversal in place of the maternal-feminine or by welcoming the divine in spirit or mind? What is, in the masculine, the relation between these two vessels? Is he able to receive woman in the reverse of herself? In the mourning for herself? Can he beckon to her and welcome her into himself once he has separated himself from her? Since he must separate himself from her in order to be able to be her place. Just as she must move toward him. If any meeting is to be possible between man and woman, each must be a place, as appropriate to and for the other, and toward which he or she may move. According to Aristotle, such a place would have to be characterized, among other things, by the dimensions of up and down, which are in fact consistently associated with the physical laws of gravitation, as well as with the economy of desire. Place would be directed up or down rather than into expansion-contraction, according to the theory elaborated about it. And to the conception of place which is still and forever Aristotle's.

"*If the place is in the thing (it must be if it is either shape or matter) place will have a place: for both the form and the indeterminate undergo change and motion along with the thing, and are not always in the same place, but are where the thing is. Hence the place will have a place.*" (210a, fifth reason; p. 357).

If place is in the thing—which is necessarily so—place is in the place. There is a *place of place*. In effect form and the indeterminate are transformed and are moved with the thing; they do not stay in the same place but stay where the thing is.

The place is in the thing, and the thing is in the place. *Place is within and without and accompanies movement*; it is its cause and accompanies it. In an extension to infinity. With each place containing the one before it. It remains to establish where the *highest point* and *the threshold* are which allow extension to take place. Is extension possible without overturning and turning over at each phase? Unless the thing is made to explode endlessly? Unless each of us returns to his or her place to find his or her cause again and then returns toward the other place, the place of the other. Which would mean that, at each phase, there were two places interdetermining each other, fitted one in the other. Two motors of place? Two causes of place? And their coming together.

Two pulses and their transformations. Of the one, of the other, and their interdeterminations. At least two. To infinity then?

Do these two pulses always fit into each other the same way? That is, with one always inside and the other out? Or sometimes in, sometimes out? Given that place is at the same time the inside and the outside, it may be imagined that the same cause does not always act within, or the same without. That, conceivably, there would be a reversal of envelopes? Which assumes that teleology is not always a forward tropism but permits reversing, turning over, crossing over. The interlacing, the embrace, of goals also as well as of the impulsion of things. Of things and of their situations? Of vessels? If so, place would mold itself from the one to the other, from the inside to the outside, from the outside to the inside. Place would twist and turn on itself. By passing through the other? Between past and future, endlessly?

If woman could be inside herself, she would have at least two things in her: herself and that for which she is a container—man and at times the child. It seems that she can be a container only for one thing, if that is her function. She is supposed only to be a container for the child, according to one moral position. She may be a container for the man. But not for herself.

Obviously, she cannot contain the child and the man in the same way. She is not the same "vessel." But, here again, the definition of vessel is not complex enough. There is a competition among:

— the container for the child,
— the container for the man,
— the container for herself.

In that competition, the first place is virtually the only place. The second is merely a sort of perforation aiming toward the first: a passage, not really a place. The third is something forbidden or impossible—set up by the excision from the *hylē* perhaps? It is necessary, Freud writes, for woman to turn away from her mother in order to enter into desire of and for man. If she remains in empathy with her mother, she remains in her

[41]

place. So her mother remains a mold for her? Back into herself she turns her mother (and) herself. She interiorizes her container-mother in herself-as-container. Between the two, she exists. And is this possible only through an idealization of the container? *Of place?* Not only of a being or of a thing but of place. Now place in this context always constitutes an inside. How is an inside to be sublimated, remembered?

There is also the question of becoming a thing for the self and for the other. Man and woman would, presumably, not become things at the same time. Perhaps woman would become a thing before *marriage*, man after? Woman would become from within, man from without?

"Further, when water is produced from air, the place has been destroyed, for the resulting body is not in the same place. What sort of destruction, then, is that?

"This concludes my statement of the reasons why space must be something, and again of the difficulties that may be raised about its essential nature." (210a; p. 357).

In this regard the question arises:

— of detumescence,

— of ejaculation,

— of the procreation of a child

in relation to the sexual act. There occurs, in fact, a destruction of place through the passage to another place. How can we work out a problematic of place that would involve not cutting or annihilation but a rhythmic becoming in relation to place? Return to the self so as to move again toward the other? Self-absorption in order to regain the tensing toward, the expansion. . . .

In fact place exists, but does it modify itself? Its essence is difficult to define. Essence, apparently, is to be reserved for generation, for engendering and for its matrix, but not for place and its modifications of place?

[42]

❦

"Since the vessel is no part of what is in it (what contains something primarily is different from what is contained), place could not be either the matter or the form of the thing contained, but must be different—for the latter, both the matter and the shape, are parts of what is contained." (210b; p. 358).

Thus matter and form are not place. If I take up the analogy with the relation between the sexes (unless thought is what is analogous to that relation? According to Freud, everything is sexuality, and thought can be nothing but a sublimation of sexuality or an anticipation of that sublimation), the womb is a container for the child (who takes form there perhaps?), the woman's sex (organ) is a container for man's sex (organ), which takes, keeps, or metamorphoses its form therein.

The female sex (organ) is neither matter nor form but *vessel*. This vessel may have its form altered, and by woman as well. Therefore she is also matter and form insofar as she is woman. With regard to the child this is less certain. It is the child that gives extension to the womb. The sexual relation is still often imagined as the relation of child to womb, stretching a fabric in order to take up residence there (but anxious about having either not enough or too much space).

In the male realm, there would be seducing, caressing, assuming a shape, spending, and then collapse into formlessness or regression to the fetal position. Do we take it that in love he is both *him* and the *plus one* of the child?

In the female realm there would be the sexual act. She gives form to the male sex (organ) and sculpts it from within. She becomes the container and the active *place* of the sexual act. Maternity is an extra. Linked to the fusion of the two: beyond form? And beyond genetics? An act more passive than passivity? Eternally confused with the sexuation of the female body. Which, for its part, would not have to be especially passive. It

[43]

seems that in the imaginary there is an inversion between the female sexual act and the maternal sexual act—modes substituted for each other. Or else the conception and the pregnancy are forgotten. The mother is considered to be "active" because she has been imagined after the birth of the child, during maternity. Hasn't woman been imagined as passive only because man would fear to lose mastery in that particular act? Which accounts for his occasional violence? So the functions of mother and wife would be inverted from the point of view of place as well as from the point of view of the man-woman functions.

"*Place is what contains*[4] *that of which it is the place.*
"*Place is no part of the thing.*
"*The primary place of a thing is neither lesser nor greater than the thing.*
"*Place can be left behind by the thing and is separable.*" (210b– 211a; p. 359).

It is hard not to think of the membranes enveloping the fetus. Since the envelope doesn't fit the thing exactly during gestation, she, and indeed he, the fetus, and the female they and the male they, are in quantitative relations that change constantly between the greater and the smaller.

We may be reminded of the skin too. But the skin is constitutive of the thing, and we cannot separate ourselves from it.

And how can we avoid remembering the sexual act as well and notably the female sex (organ) as a place? In the confusion it potentially sets up with man's first "home" but also with his *skin*. The woman's sex (organ) is supposed in some way to serve as skin to the man's sex organ, to man himself. Without access to that other dimension: the *mucous*. Dimension of the sexual act? Of its approach, its economy, its communion beyond skins.

Up and down are properties of all places. Astonishingly there

---

[4](In the French Budé edition used by Irigaray, this phrase is rendered as "l'enveloppe première."—Tr.)

is no suggestion here of a *spherical* place where no clear-cut distinction between up and down would obtain. Notwithstanding, sexuality partakes in the up and the down, in rising and falling. Bodies in this context are sometimes lighter, sometimes heavier, sometimes warmer, sometimes colder, and so on. But bodies also face the issue of fitting one inside the other, without thereby altering the other dimensions. Can this be understood as the constitution, together, of a spherical or almost spherical form?

Research about place is always governed by movement according to place. If, in regard to "heaven," more thought is given to the fact that it is "in place" than to anything else, this is because "it is in constant movement." Movement can either be "locomotion" or "increase and diminution." These both in fact mean a change of place. While remaining within the womb, the child changes place. While remaining within the woman, the man changes place. Both are smaller or greater in relation to the envelope which keeps them inside. Which is also them, in fact, as well as the relation between the two.

"We say that a thing is in the world [dans le ciel] in the sense of in place, because it is in the air, and the air is in the world; and when we say it is in the air, we do not mean it is in every part of the air, but that it is in the air because of the surface of the air which surrounds it; for if all the air were its place, the place of a thing would not be equal to the thing—which it is supposed to be, and which the primary place in which the thing is actually is." (211a; p. 359).

If it is the whole of the air that is place, each thing will not be equal to its place. Yet this equality would be the immediate place of the thing.

"When what surrounds [l'enveloppe], then, is not separate from the thing, but is in continuity with it, the thing is said to be in what surrounds it, not in the sense of in place, but as a part in a whole." (211a; p. 359).

[45]

Can this be understood of the *body* and in its relation to the *skin*? In a different way from the *fetus* in its relation with the first enveloping membranes and the umbilical cord. Even though the fetus is a continuum with the body it is in, even though it passes from a certain kind of continuity to another through the mediation of fluids: blood, milk. . . . The fetus has a peculiar status which can mean that the child fantasizes itself as a part of that whole that is the mother's body. And it is true that he belongs to that body and is fed by that body until he comes into the world. That part of the whole, of a whole, that the fetus partially is will affect the fantasy of the penis also. Whence the fantasies of castration, perhaps? If the penis did not present itself in fantasy as forming a part of another whole, it would not be imagined as separate from the whole to which it "belongs." Obviously, the movement of the penis is partially linked to another whole. Is it double? For the self and for the other. But why is the temporary end of a certain movement, or its suspension, called castration or separation of a body unless man desires to become once more part of a matrical body? Which is impossible. On the other hand, there are times when that relation of places in the sexual act gives rise to a transgression of the envelope, to a porousness, a perception of the other, a fluidity. And so it becomes possible to imagine that generation of a certain kind might occur by crossing membranes and sharing humors with the other.

"*But when the thing is separate and in contact, it is primarily in the inner surface of the surrounding body, and this surface is neither a part of what is in it nor yet greater than its extension, but equal to it; for the extremities of things which touch are coincident.*

"*Further, if one body is in continuity with another, it is not moved* in *that but* with *that. On the other hand it is moved* in *that if it is separate. It makes no difference whether what contains is moved or not.*" (211a; p. 359).

When the envelope is separate and simply in contact, the body is immediately inside the outermost surface of the envelope, which neither forms a part of its contents nor is bigger than the interval of extension of the body, but equal to it; for the extremities of the things in contact are joined.

Once again, the whole issue of the fetus's relation to place (or of the point to the boundary limiting its growth?) and of the male sex (organ) to the female sex (organ) is bound up with this problematic of how the body fits the envelope. Fitting and separate—is this the horizon for the meeting of the sexes in its different dimensions? With reversals of envelopes and envelopings almost to infinity?

Or else:

— Is it possible here to think of the genetic (?) capital received and of the skin, of the skins joined to this genetic capital. "My" skin, in theory, corresponds to my growth.

— In gestation, there will always be a gap, an interval between the body that is in the envelope and the envelope itself which will more or less fit that body, and the amniotic fluid which separates the two.

— The envelope as here defined can also be related to some "ideal" sexual act. Since the elasticity of the tissues allows an approach to that ideal. (But there are transmutations, sublimations, and transfers in the physiology of the envelopes with endless growing and unfolding . . .).

What is place? Shape? Matter? Interval between the two? Extremities? *"There are just four things of which place must be one."* (211b; pp. 359–60).

Two of these it obviously cannot be:

—*Place is not form.* By the property it has of surrounding, of being an envelope, form appears to be place: the boundaries of what surrounds and what is surrounded are the same. In actual fact, these are two boundaries but not of the same being. Form is the boundary of the thing; the place, the boundary of the surrounding body.

— *Place is not the interval ("some sort of extension between the extremities").* Whereas the container remains, that which is contained changes. The interval which is intermediary *between the boundaries* appears to be something insofar as it is independent of the displaced body. This is not so, but it happens *in the place of one body or other*, provided it be one of those bodies who can move and whose nature it is to enter into contact.

The change of the body and the modification of the interval represent an important issue in the economy of desire. The *locomotion toward* and *reduction in interval* are the movements of desire (even by expansion-retraction). The greater the desire, the greater the tendency to overcome the interval while at the same time retaining it. An interval that might perhaps be occupied by the transformed body? Overcoming the interval is the aim of desire, the cause of locomotion. The interval approaches zero when skins come into contact. It goes beyond zero when a passage occurs to the mucous. Or a transgression of touch through the skin. Given that the problem of desire is to suppress the interval without suppressing the other. Since desire can eat up place, either by regressing into the other on the intrauterine model or annihilating the existence of the other in one way or another. If desire is to subsist, a double place is necessary, a double envelope. Or else God as subtending the interval, pushing the interval toward and into infinity. The irreducible. Opening up the universe and all beyond it. In this sense, the interval would produce place.

"*The extension between the extremities is thought to be something, because what is contained and separate may often be changed while the container [l'enveloppe] remains the same (as water may be poured from a vessel)—the assumption being that the extension [l'intervalle] is something over and above the body displaced. But there is no such extension. One of the bodies which change places and are naturally capable of being in contact with the container falls in—whichever it may chance to be.*" (211b; p. 360).

Does sexuality encounter that aporia or that question in which it competes with the question of God?

Certainly, apart from the fact that, in the eroticism of the different senses or thresholds of the body, the interval remains in play as place, or the possibility of place, it is particularly insistent with regard to the *lips* (and perhaps the eyelids?). And to everything in the female sex which figures the abyss. Oscillations between the infinitely small and the infinitely large?

The womb, for its part, would figure rather as place. Though of course what unfolds in the womb unfolds in function of an interval, a cord, that is never done away with. Whence perhaps the infinite nostalgia for that first home? The interval cannot be done away with.[5]

". . . *all the portions of the two together will play the same part in the whole which was previously played by all the water in the vessel; at the same time the place too will be undergoing change; so that there will be another place which is the place of the place, and many places will be coincident. There is not a different place of the part, in which it is moved, when the whole vessel changes its place: it is always the same: for it is in the place where they are that the air and the water (or the parts of the water) succeed each other, not in that place in which they come to be, which is part of the place which is the place of the whole world [du ciel entier].*" (211b; p. 360).

The elements fill the universe. They can potentially be transformed one into another, but they always fill the whole up

[5] See Luce Irigaray, *La Croyance même* (Paris: Galilée, 1983). (Irigaray also includes this essay in *Sexes and Genealogies*, trans. Gillian C. Gill [New York: Columbia University Press, 1993].—Tr.)

equally. The universe is conceived as a closed vessel, the receptacle for all the elements.

"The matter, too, might seem to be place, at least if we consider it in what is at rest and is thus separate but in continuity. For just as in change of quality there is something which was formerly black and is now white, or formerly soft and now hard—this is just why we say that the matter exists—so place, because it presents a similar phenomenon, is thought to exist—only in the one case we say so because what was air is now water, in the other because where air formerly was there is now water." (211b; p. 360).

The proof of place is thus seen to lie in the transformation of elements in place.

Place necessarily is *"the boundary of the containing body [corps enveloppant] at which it is in contact with the contained body [corps enveloppé]. (By the contained body is meant what can be moved by way of locomotion.)"* (212a; p. 361).

The boundary of the "containing body" can be understood of the womb. If it has no outside, desire can go on to infinity. Is this the way with the desire for God that does not know the outside of the universe?

But sexual desire that goes toward the womb and no longer returns to it also goes toward infinity since it never touches the boundary of the "containing body." Instead of perceiving the body that contains it *hic et nunc*, it goes toward another container. Instead of moving across the actual container in the direction of the other through porosity, it remains nostalgic for another home.

So there is never any idea that the boundary of the containing body might be the skin, while passing through the mucous membranes and through the body and the flesh. The boundary of the containing body might be the bodily identity of woman, reborn and touched anew by inner communion, and not destroyed by nostalgia for a regression in utero. The dissociation of love and desire would, in this case, have little meaning, nor would the sexual have an amoral, or nonethical, character. On the contrary, the sexual *act* would turn into the act whereby the other gives new form, birth, incarnation to the self. Instead of implying the downfall of the body, it takes part in the body's renaissance. And there is no other equivalent act, in this sense. Most divine of acts. Whereby man makes woman feel her body as place. Not only her vagina and her womb but her body. He places her within her body and within a macrocosm, releasing her from her potential adherence to the cosmic through her participation in a microsociety.

As man re-creates woman from outside, from inside-outside, he re-places himself outside, as an actor outside, a creator outside. By actively putting himself outside, he re-sculpts a body for himself. By using a tool? He reconstructs his own body as a result of engendering the body of the other. By using his hand, his penis—which is not merely a tool of pleasure, but a truly useful tool of alliance, incarnation, creation.

Woman, insofar as she is a container, is never a closed one. Place is never closed. The boundaries touch against one another while still remaining open. And can they do so without necessarily touching the boundaries of the body contained? There are two touches between boundaries; and these are not the same: the touch of one's body at the threshold; the touch of the contained other. There is also the internal touch of the body of the child, with mother and child being separated by one envelope or several. Within this container the child moves. Is it possible to speak of locomotion? It seems not. Where would the child move to? Toward the place that nourishes him, toward the exit that leads from one place to another place? And again toward that movement of growth within the place?

"Hence the place of a thing is the innermost motionless boundary of what contains it." (212a; p. 361).

[51]

An Ethics of Sexual Difference

ɞ

"If then a body has another body outside it and containing it [qui l'enveloppe], it is in place, and if not, not." (212a, 5; p. 361).

It seems that a fetus would be in a place. And man's penis for as long as it is inside the woman. Woman is in the house, but this is not the same type of place as a living bodily site. On the other hand, place, in her, is in place, not only as organs but as vessel or receptacle. It is place twice over: as mother and as woman.

"That is why, even if there were to be water which had not a container, the parts of it will be moved." (212a, 5; p. 361).

A certain representation of feminine jouissance corresponds to this water flowing without a container. A doubling, sought after by man, of a female *placelessness.* She is assigned to be place without occupying a place. Through her, place would be set up for man's use but not hers. Her jouissance is meant to "resemble" the flow of whatever is in the place that she is when she contains, contains herself. "Wine," perhaps, that man might spill out in the sexual act? Elixir of ambrosia, and of place itself.

Is there some jouissance other than that of place? Is this not the jouissance which goes from the most elementary to the most subtle? From in utero to heaven, from earth to heaven, from hell to heaven, and so on. And isn't food a matter of introducing something into a place, and of being able to keep it in, or not? The body and foods play roles that escape the "subject." For the most part.

Reduction to fluidity would seem, then, to be the non-procreative aspect of female jouissance. Separation of place from that which it contained? Of place. Separation of the container from its contents so that it/he/she is left empty? For the other. As well as for that other "solid": the child. Division of woman into two: on the one hand, she is habitually devalued in relation to the fluid; on the other hand, she is valued in relation to the solid. But this valuation process is ambiguous as far as she is concerned since it deprives her of the subtlest part of herself: place as such, the place she contains, invisibly. And which, in most cases, is diffused without being noticed? Or is diffused profanely. Even unconsciously and involuntarily.

This place, the production of intimacy, is in some manner a transmutation of earth into heaven, here and now. Providing she remembers? An alchemist of the sexual and one who tries to keep the sexual away from repetition, degradation. Attempts to keep it and sublimate it. *Between.* In the interval of time, of times. Weaving the veil of time, the fabric of time, time with space, time in space. Between past and future, future and past, place in place. Invisible. Its vessel? Its container? The soul of the soul?

A second container, imperceptible and yet there, offered up to man in the sexual relation. How fitting if the container were offered back to her in a sort of irradiation outside of her "grace" from within. She would be re-contained with place in place. Thanks to her partner. A kind of permanent assumption, perhaps? Or else the place she has woven in her womb would return to her as place of her conception? She would be re-contained by that weaving of space-time that she has secretly conceived.

Nothing more spiritual, in this regard, than female sexuality. Always working to produce a place of transcendence for the sensible, which can become a destructive net, or else find itself, remain, in endless becoming. Accompanying cosmic time. Between man's time and the time of the universe. Still faithful to the one and seeking to find a rhythm in the other, perhaps?

Unfortunately, the two are often cut apart. Those two rhythms are not only no longer harmonious but are cut off from one another. Does this produce false gods and false hells? To avoid this, an alchemy of female desire is needed.

"*The parts of it will be moved (for one part is contained in another) while the whole will be moved in one sense, but not in another.*" (212a, 5; p. 361).

Do the parts of the whole envelop one another mutually? Is there no part that destroys another? Do the parts of the body contain one another mutually? Is there no part that destroys another? In love, it would be fitting if the parts of the whole—the union of man and woman—enveloped one another *mutually* and did not destroy one another's envelopes. How fitting if the two-way journeys from the one to the other became places for enveloping. If the portions of place traversed in order to move away and then back were to become space-times that mutually recovered and were not eliminated, annihilated, used up to provide fuel for other kinds of locomotion, or transformed into voids, separations, rather than bridges. Between the one and the other, there should be mutual enveloping in movement. For the one and the other move around within a whole. And often the one and the other destroy the place of the other, believing in this way to have the whole; but they possess or construct only an illusory whole and destroy the meeting and the interval (of attraction) between the two. The world is destroyed in its essential symbol: the copula of the sex act. It is opened up to the abyss and not to welcome generation, the search for creation.

"For as a whole it does not simultaneously change its place, though it will be moved in a circle: for this place is the place of its parts. And some things are moved, not up and down, but in a circle; others up and down, such things namely as admit of condensation and rarefaction." (212b, 5; p. 361).

The whole, in fact, does not change place but moves in a circle. The universe turns round and round? Moves around? And the love between man and woman likewise, had it not been brutally cut into two (see Plato, *Symposium*). According to that story, man and woman were once joined together in such a way that they rolled around, locked in embrace. Then they were split apart, but endlessly each seeks to find the lost half and embrace once more. Unless the one or the other claims to be the whole? And constructs his world into a closed circle. Total? Closed to

the other. And convinced that there is no access to outside except by opening up a wound. Having no part in the construction
of love, or of beauty, or the world.

Could it be that anything that moves in a circle moves in
relation to another? In two directions? With a place of attraction.
A place of place. Where bodies embrace? Both in and not in the
same place: with the one being in the other that contains. But,
by wishing to give, he or she constitutes the other as receptacle?
Unless he refuses. (Cf. Nietzsche, "On the Great Longing," in
Thus Spoke Zarathustra: "I gave you all," but "which of us has to
be thankful? Should not the giver be thankful that the receiver
received," formed himself into a *place*. "Oh my soul, I gave you
all; I thank you for having received," for having become place.)[6]

Does man become place in order to receive and because he has
received female jouissance? How? Does woman become place
because she has received male jouissance? How? How does one
make the transition here from physics to metaphysics? From the
physical receptacle for the penis to the enveloping of a receptacle
that is less tangible or visible, but which makes place?

[6] Friedrich Nietzsche, *Thus Spoke Zarathustra*, trans. Walter Kaufmann in *The
Portable Nietzsche* (New York: Viking Press, 1964), p. 333. (Irigaray's text
combines exact citation with paraphrase.—Tr.)

❦ II

Love of Self

Love of Self?

The expression "love of self" raises certain possibilities, poses many questions: problems of envelopes, of the doubling of the self and within the self, of the positioning of the self and within the self.

Love of self. The status of this *of* is complex. Who is loving whom? Or who is loving a part of whom? How in this case is the relationship between subject and object to be determined? The relation between two different subjects?

Love of self. I am supposed to relate to my self, but how? The *I* is supposed to relate to the self, but how? By what mediation? What means? What instrument? And what are the two terms: the subject of love and the loved self?

Love of self creates a particular movement, a kind of play between active and passive, in which, between me and me, there takes place this double relationship, neither active nor truly passive. I do not set a completely inchoate material in motion. The material is, in some measure, already given. Neither the subject nor the self is fixed in its position or its given, otherwise the two would be separated without any possibility of love. A liaison takes place which corresponds to no other coded or codable operation: neither active nor passive nor middle-passive,[1] even if this operation is the closest.

Love of self raises a question for language, a question for the subject, for the world, for the other, for the god(s).

Love of self represents an enigma, an impossibility, sometimes a taboo. Often, in this era of sexual subjectivism, all that remains of love of self is a kind of masturbation, certain modes of pleasure and jouissance. But love? This question seems to be much more difficult and is not necessarily to be confused with questions of pleasure or of jouissance. Love of self is a question asked of *eros*, of *agape*, of eroticism, of death.

How can I love myself? Who is who in this love? I relate to myself, I affect myself, I am affected by myself. That which affects me is an attribute of mine. But who or what separates the one who loves from the one who is loved? And, if both of these are separated, who or what allows them to come close again?

Love of Self: The Male Version

The male version of love of self often takes the form or sounds the note of nostalgia for a maternal-feminine that has been forever lost. Insofar as man or men are concerned, it seems that auto-affection is possible only through a search for the first home. Man's self-affect depends on the woman who has given him being and birth, who has born/e him, enveloped him, warmed him, fed him. Love of self would seemingly take the form of a long *return* to and through the other. A unique female other, who is forever lost and must be sought in many others, an

---

[1] (In English grammars of ancient Greek, the "middle-passive" [*moyen-passif*] is more commonly known as the middle voice: a verbal form that is neither active nor passive, it is used to convey the subject's performance of an action in which he or she is implicated or which is performed in his or her own interest and, as such, often carries a reflexive sense.—Tr.)

infinite number of others. The distance for this return can be conquered by the transcendence of God. The (female) other who is sought and cherished may be assimilated to the unique god. The (female) other is mingled or confused with God or the gods.

Love of self, for man, seems to oscillate among three poles:
— nostalgia for the mother-womb entity,
— quest for God through the father,
— love of one part of the self (conforming principally to the dominant sexual model).

According to this economy, the female either becomes the unique one or becomes the infinite series of one plus one plus one . . . parts of a broken whole.

There remain two other terms that we would need to distinguish from the three already mentioned:
— love of self through the *same other man*,
— love of self through the *other same woman*.

Let love be that which can be given-returned as affection for self *through the other here and now*:

1. according to a durational time that would be neither pure nostalgia for the past nor an appeal to the future with regard to the unique;

2. neither a fragmentation that puts its reassemblage off to some past or future day (a problematic assemblage that relates more to *space* and which in sexual language seems to be translated into partial drives and the regrouping of those drives into genitality), nor a kind of shilly-shallying that puts off until tomorrow its need to discharge and recharge (a process that puts in play the relation to time, the same relation implied also in the cathexis of language or speech), to accumulate and return to zero;

3. nor a simple part of the self in the other of the same or of the other, but a voyage through the other that returns to the self and constitutes the self through the space-time of nostalgia and of hope.

[*61*]

How is this *self* to remain open into the present? Open enough? Still susceptible to the affect of the *I*. Closed and enveloped enough to make a self. Separate enough so that I can affect it and be affected by it. Close enough or approachable enough for affect to be possible. The *of* (love *of* self) always a little biunivocal. Transitive and reflexive. Doubly transitive. Sufficiently two and one.

But neither on the model

— *of the smaller and the bigger* (the parental model, which is at times carried over into the relation to the divine),

— nor of the *part and the whole.*

In the love of self, there is a *two* which is not really a *two*— given that the *I* and the *self* are at once separate and not separate.

Love of Self: The Female Version

The female version of the love of self is as yet more difficult to realize in our tradition. Though, theoretically, shouldn't it be easier? Easier and more difficult.

Historically, the female has been used in the constitution of man's love of self. Not that that love has been or is today simple to establish. Far from it. Not that it can or could be taken as self-evident. It involved—as I have already said—nostalgia, faith and hope, returning to the past, suspending the beyond, the inaccessible transcendent, a recourse to the existence of the soul, labor, creation of work, and, primarily, of one particular work, the family: home, wife, and children, extensions of the self. Many things were needed to achieve a love of self that was always threatened, always in danger, always unstable, often wounded or ridiculously inflated: lack of confidence metamorphoses into a show of overconfidence, a social or intellectual pretension that deceives no one, especially not women. Love of self—or rather its lack or its precariousness—gives way to a defensive sexuality that tends, in particular, to exaggerate how necessary an erection is in seduction. An erection that is always threatened, always failing, whose deficiencies will be compensated for through the *reproduction of the child*. Because he is almost always in a state of narcissistic insecurity in sexual relations, man projects insecurity onto others, like a master who loads his problems onto the shoulders of his slave or his "thing." Valuing woman insofar as he values himself—in her role as *mother*, correlative to his fatherhood, *proof of his potency*.

Love of self, for a man, is not self-evident. Different circumstances come to his assistance. His sex (organ) presents itself as something *external*, through which he can love himself—although this has its own dangers, its own threat of loss or fragmentation. All the same, that organ is on show, on exhibit, presented or represented, even in its movements. This is not true for the female sex organs. Because his sex is on display, man will make an infinite number of substitutes for it; through things that exist, things he creates, objects, women—thereby parceling out his desire. But each time at the expense of one deception or other, he believes he loves, is loved, in a virtually definitive way.

Love of self on the female side is a more complex experience. The female has always served the self-love of man, obviously. But there is also the fact that the female does not have the same relation to exteriority as the male. Woman is loved/loves herself through the children she *gives birth to*. That she brings *out*. She herself cannot watch herself desiring (except through another woman? Who is not herself? One of the dangers of love between women is the confusion in their identities, the lack of respect for or of perception of differences). For her self, something is missing in the presentation or representation of her desire. And of her "end." The (indefinite) series one plus one plus one, etc. (masculine and/or feminine) does not interest her as much as it does the male. Because she *participates in the maternal*? Because, still, she is the unique one? Or else because her desire does not speak according to the same economy. As Antigone says: he wants everything right away or death. Not *and* death. *Or*: death.

[*63*]

For the female, everything right away is not the equivalent of death. It is more like a quest for the infinite of life. An openness on the infinite in jouissance. Man sets the infinite in a *transcendence* that is always deferred to the beyond, even if it be the beyond of the concept. Woman sets it in an *expanse* of jouissance here and now right away. Body-expanse that tries to *give itself exteriority, to give itself to exteriority*, to give itself in an unpunctuated space-time that is also not orgastic in the limited sense of that word. To give itself in a space-time without end. Or very resistant to definition. Quite literally, if man—or she herself—did not have to work, if she did not have to feed herself and *procreate* (which is an interruption in her jouissance, or in her other jouissance), woman could live in love indefinitely. Which accounts for the difficulty she has in interrupting the act of love. She always wants *more, encore,* we are told by certain psychoanalysts (Jacques Lacan in particular) who equate this *more* with pathology. In fact, this *more* is the condition of sexuate female desire. Impossible, no doubt, to satisfy in everyday life. But not pathological for all that. Whereas man must live out the pain and experience the impossibility of being cut off from and in *space* (being born, leaving the mother), woman lives out the painful or impossible experience of being cut off from or in *time*. (Is this their empirico-transcendental chiasmus?). Man is separated from that primary space which, it appears, is everything to him. He lives out a kind of exile between the *never more* and the *not yet.* Woman can occupy the place of the spatial. She is assisted in this role by her relation to the cyclical. But not in the traditional act of love (in which, notably, she has no access to language as temporal scansion). Even if she extends infinitely into space, and thereby risks losing time (except, perhaps, for eternity? In this regard, one should reread Nietzsche's "Seven Seals" in *Zarathustra*), this is because her sexuality does not have to obey the imperatives and risks of erection and detumescence. In some sense her jouissance is a result of indefinite *touching*. The *thresholds* do not necessarily mark a limit, the end of an act. She can take part in the man's act, or even produce it, without ever achieving her own act. In the act of love, she finds herself more or less expanded, more or less deeply touched, more or less unfolded in her desire of the moment. Time is not measured in the same way for her as for man. A sentence without a period? A musical phrase that would never end? An expanse extending on and on forever. A horizon forever open, closed up only with difficulty, as a result of that other punctuation or rhythm.[2]

As she travels, she has trouble marking the different stages! She lacks, notably, the power to fold back around her the dwelling which she is. The power to clothe herself not only in the garments of seduction for the sake of man, or any other, but also in something that would speak her jouissance, her sexuate body, and would offer her the clothing and protection *outside* of that home which she is *inside*. Tradition places her within the home, sheltered in the home. But that home, which is usually paid for by man's labor (this is the law of the land, as well as the religious law) encloses her, places her in *internal exile* (does that mean man is in *external* exile?) unless she is able, in some other way, to take on the envelope of her "own" desire, the garb of her "own" jouissance, of her "own" love. Withholding all these so that they are not cut off at the end of the act of love, are unaffected by the rhythm of detumescence, so that her body is not ripped into pieces. As can happen when her partner or she herself over-cathects one part of her body and spells her and it out: one plus one plus one plus one. . . .

It is essential that she no longer depend on man's return for her self love. Or at least not absolutely. But a whole history separates her from the love of herself. Freud claims in his theory of sexuality that woman has to put love for her mother and for

[2]In this regard, see what is said about *touch* in "Volume-Fluidity," in Luce Irigaray, *Speculum of the Other Woman*, trans. Gillian C. Gill (Ithaca: Cornell University Press, 1985), pp. 227–40, and in "When Our Lips Speak Together," in Luce Irigaray, *This Sex Which Is Not One*, trans. Catherine Porter with Carolyn Burke (Ithaca: Cornell University Press, 1985), pp. 205–18.

herself aside in order to begin to love men. She has to stop loving herself in order to love a man who, for his part, would be able, and indeed expected, to continue to love himself. He has to renounce his mother, in order to love himself, for example. She has to renounce her mother *and* her auto-eroticism in order not to love herself anymore. In order to love man alone. To enter into desire for the man-father. Which does not necessarily mean that she loves him. How could she love him without loving herself?

This is one of the questions uncovered—sometimes only as a negative—when women take consciousness of themselves. Women can no longer love or desire the other man if they cannot love themselves. Women are no longer willing to be the guardians of love, especially when it is an improbable or even pathological love. Women want to find themselves, discover themselves and their own identity. Which is why they are seeking each other out, loving each other, associating with each other. At least until the world changes. As the historical moment indispensable for women, as the period necessary to achieve love?

It Takes at Least Two to Love

Until the present day, in most cases, love took place in the *One.* Two merely formed a one. However, even when love manages to achieve this goal of oneness, it can do so only in exceptional cases, after great effort, and never by decree. You will be as one, the law decrees. But the law doesn't say how this can work. It creates an obligation without showing us how to comply.

What we need is to discover how *two* can be made which one day could become a *one* in that third which is love, for example.

Currently there is a kind of *one* built on a division of labor, of goods, of discourse, a *one* which is merely an enslaving complementarity: yet, love cannot but be free. A kind of *one*, moreover, which is incarnated only in the child—thus trapping the three terms in an alliance which is no alliance. If the *one* of love is ever to be achieved, we have to discover the *two*.

This presupposes that several tasks have been successfully tackled:
1. *No more hierarchy of maternal and paternal functions* which reduces them to the effect of the division of labor: the reproduction of the child and the work force, on the one hand, the reproduction of society and of symbolic and cultural capital, on the other.
2. *No more dissociation of love and eroticism.*
   This very often correlates with the division and hierarchy of parental functions.

   This way love becomes a perpetual tragedy, a sad charity, or a greedy devotion (a form of *agape* without *eros*, perhaps?).

   This way love gets reduced to technocratic sexuality, always hunting for new techniques or targets, ending up bored and expecting happiness only in the world beyond.
3. *The possibility that the female could be many*; that women would form a social group.

If women have no access to society and culture:
— they are abandoned to a state of neither knowing each other nor loving each other, or themselves;
— they have no way to mediate the operations of sublimation;
— love remains impossible for them.

If love for two is to happen, it has to go through the many. However, since society is organized by and for men in our traditions, women are unable to work with plurals. Women have to constitute a social entity if love and cultural fecundity are to take place. This does not mean that it is entirely as men that women come into today's systems of power, but rather that women need to establish new values that correspond to *their* creative capacities. Society, culture, discourse would thereby be recognized as *sexuate* and not as the monopoly on universal value of a single sex—one that has no awareness of the way the body and its morphology are imprinted upon imaginary and symbolic creations.

4. *The existence of a female divine.*

Innerness, self-intimacy, for a woman, can be established or re-established only through the mother-daughter, daughter-mother relationship which woman re-plays for herself. Herself with herself, in advance of any procreation. This way she becomes capable of respecting herself in her childhood and in her maternal creative function. This is one of the most difficult gestures for our culture. According to our traditions, which for centuries have stayed faithful to a God-father who engenders a God-son by means of a virgin-mother, the maternal function serves to mediate the generation of the son. This function, which is certainly divine, sets up no genealogy of the divine among women, and in particular between mother and daughter. A traditional reading of the Gospels in fact places very little stress on the good relations between Mary and Anne, Mary and Elizabeth, etc., Mary and the other women. Even though this corner of society does form a part of the "Good News," few texts or sermons transmit or teach its message. And few New Testament commentaries dwell on the attention that Christ always paid to women. Everything is laid at the door of the Father's glory, or the son's, with no regard for the scriptures themselves. And however many seeds may lie dormant in religious texts, invariably the mature organism grows in the direction of God the Father and not of a goddess mother or woman, mother and woman. The very word *goddess*, in fact, always seems to have the implication of one of many, not one unique one. For centuries the One has remained entrusted to God, even though this longing for the unique is a specifically male nostalgia, derived from man's desire for the lost womb. With God the Father substituting for the return to and into the mother which can never take place.

It remains true that this *bridge* is theoretically unavailable to women. They supposedly lack the horizon and the foundation needed to progress between past and future. Their present would forever be an offshoot of man's time and eternity, since there is no transcendental made to their measure, since they have to make one for themselves. A transcendental which leaves them free to embrace the maternal while giving them back their childhood at the same time. A transcendental, moreover, that surrounds them and envelops them in their jouissance. Clothing them in that *porousness* and that *mucous* that they are. Opening up for them the space-time of all that they lovingly bring into bloom.

Love of self for the female would thus require
— detachment from what is, from the situation in which woman has traditionally been placed;
— love for the child that she once was, that she still is, and a shared enveloping of the child by the mother and of the mother by the child;
— an openness, *in addition* to that mutual love, which allows access to difference.

This means that the enveloping between mother and daughter, daughter and mother, among women, must not become closure, enclosure while protecting the one "for the other's sake" in a state of seduction or bondage that annihilates any possibility of subjecthood. Given that love of the same, within the same, is a form of innerness that can open to the other without loss of self or of the other in the bottomlessness of an abyss.

For a woman, the question of *who loves whom?* in the love of self seems even more mysterious than for a man. Because a woman cannot place herself as an object for herself. And because, unsettled by this lack of a possible "position," she allows herself to be placed by the other—man or mother. She herself does not love herself as object. She may try to love herself as innerness. But she cannot see herself. She has to succeed in loving the invisible and the memory of a touch that is never seen, that often she feels only in pain because she is unable to perceive its place, its "substance," its qualities. A touch without tool or object, except for the test, the experience, of innerness. From within, and from her potential passage from inside to outside, from outside to inside, and all this without the involvement of anything that moves from one place to another, but only a place of passage, and its movement.

In psychoanalytic categories, this path has not been thought through. Nor even imagined? Except in its pathological symptoms. It is left in the shadow of the *pre-object*, and in the suffering and abandonment of the fusional state which fails to emerge as a subject. No space-time is available for experiencing it. Traditionally spacing is created, or occupied, by man, child, housework, cooking. Not by the woman herself *for herself*. And when she is placed as an object by and for man, love of self is arrested in its development. She needs to accede to a love of herself, an affection of and in the invisible which can be expressed in that which touches itself without consummation.

If an analogy were sought in that which already exists as a statute of representation, this love of self might perhaps be compared to the *icon* insofar as that differs from the *idol* and the *fetish*. In the icon, the passage from inside to outside occurs through the insistence of the invisible within visibility: the icon irradiates the invisible, and its gaze seems to gaze on the visible from out of the invisible, gaze of the gaze beyond our usual (?) perceptions. The idol, however, attracts the gaze but blinds it with a brilliance that bars access to the invisible; it flashes; it dazzles, it does not lead toward another threshold, another texture of gaze, of world, of meaning. Rather it destroys the horizonal perspective. The fetish is meant to be the place where innerness is guarded, or at least guaranteed; some "thing" precious would lie hidden in it, precious because hidden, which does not mean invisible, nor even existent; the fetish would have us believe in a valuable mystery or a mysterious value; it would set up or destroy in seduction the power of the invisible. In painting, only the icon would speak and not speak the invisible, like a reality that *must be recognized* and not merely as the reverse side or other side of the visible, but as its texture, its shelter, here and now; which doesn't simply mean within reach of hand or tool: another dimension would be involved, of the gaze, of speaking, of flesh.

As our tradition has it, this dimension is covered over, swallowed up, or relegated to the beyond. Which places the female in an oblivion that entails the abyss, the abandonment and the dispersion of the other-man. Lost, nostalgic, man entrusts to woman his memory; he makes woman the keeper of his house, his sex (organ), his history. But he is unable to establish any long-lasting love of self. And this puts the maternal-feminine in the position of keeping that love without its loving itself. Woman is meant to assimilate love to herself as her preserve, without any return for her, without any love of her which might offer her access to a space-time "of her own."

Scarcely does she know herself, scarcely does she begin to glimpse nostalgia for herself—her *odyssey*. To be able to tell her tears from those of Ulysses. Not because they were weeping the same loving tears, but because she took part in his quest for love for himself. Which does not come to the same thing. That might happen if woman also went in quest of "her own" love. Successfully accomplishing her journey.

Preventing the other—man or woman—from pursuing his or her voyage is useless.

It takes two to love. To know how to separate and how to come back together. Each to go, both he and she, in quest of self, faithful to the quest, so they may greet one another, come close, make merry, or seal a covenant.

Wonder:

A Reading of Descartes,

The Passions of the Soul

We need to reread Descartes a little and remember or learn about the role of movement in the passions. We should also think about the fact that all philosophers—except for the most recent ones? and why is this so?—have always been physicists and have always supported or accompanied their metaphysical research with cosmological research, whether it concerns the macrocosm or the microcosm. It is only lately that this grounding of research has been abandoned. Is this because an autonomous epistemology has been set up in the sciences?

This scission between the physical sciences and thought no doubt represents that which threatens thought itself. Splitting our life, our bodies, our language, our breath into several worlds. Dispersing us into atoms or circuits of energy which no longer find common ground. Neither primary philosophy nor God provides a roof for our potential to dwell as mortals. And often we survive by regressing to schemas prior to *ideation*, the patient work of the architecture of ideality: sociofamilial stratifications of desire in the form of the *ideal ego* or the *ego ideal*, which bring about a return to religiosity, slogans, publicity, terror, etc. All forms of passively experienced passions in which the subject is enclosed, constrained, deprived of its roots, whether vegetal and earthly or ideal and heavenly. Sap no longer circulates between the beginning and the end of its incarnation. And there is no *window*, no sense remaining open on, or with, the world, the Other, the other. In order to dwell within it, transform it. What is lacking there in terms of the passions is *wonder*.

"*When the first encounter with some object surprises us, and we judge it to be new or very different from what we formerly knew, or from what we supposed that it ought to be, that causes us to wonder and be surprised; and because that may happen before we in any way know whether this object is agreeable to us or is not so, it appears to me that wonder is the first of all the passions; and it has no opposite, because if the object which presents itself has nothing in it that surprises us, we are in no wise moved regarding it, and we consider it without passion.*" (René Descartes, *The Passions of the Soul*, art. 53, p. 358).[1]

Wonder is the motivating force behind mobility in all its dimensions. From its most vegetative to its most sublime functions, the living being has need of wonder to move. Things must be good, beautiful, and desirable for all the senses and meaning, the sense that brings them together. And, if one admits that one's senses are hierarchized (and in space-time), it matters for "man" to find a vital speed, a growth speed that is compatible with all his senses and meanings, and for him to know how to stop in order to rest, to leave an interval between himself and the other, to look toward, to contemplate—*to wonder*. Wonder being an action that is both active and passive. The ground or inner secret of genesis, of creation? The place of the union or the alliance of power and act. Perhaps man is at the end of his growth? Or thinks he is? Is he turning back on himself to complete a cycle, as do Nietzsche and Heidegger?

[1] Page references following quotations from René Descartes, *The Passions of the Soul*, are to *The Philosophical Works of Descartes*, vol. 1, trans. E. S. Haldane and G. R. T. Ross (Cambridge: Cambridge University Press, 1931; reprinted, Dover, 1955). (Following the usage of Haldane and Ross, Descartes's term *l'admiration* is rendered as "wonder."—Tr.)

But this turning back results either in regeneration by means of reimplantation in fertile ground—man having exhausted his resources would rest in order to replenish his land—or else in a series of increasingly accelerated turns. This ends up purifying the good of the bad, or destroying the whole. As long as we are embodied, we cannot go beyond a certain rhythm of growth. We must always keep on accelerating and braking. Both. With and without the world. Both. With and without the other. Both. And doesn't the machine unceasingly threaten to destroy us through the speed of its acceleration?

Unless there is wonder? Can we look at, contemplate, wonder at the machine from a place where it does not see us?

Still, the other—he or she—can look at us. And it is important for us to be able to wonder at him or her even if he or she is looking at us. Overcome the spectacle, the visible, make a place for us to inhabit, a reason and a means of moving, a way of stopping ourselves, of going forward or backward through wonder.

This first passion is indispensable not only to life but also or still to the creation of an ethics. Notably of and through sexual difference. This other, male or female, should *surprise* us again and again, appear to us as *new*, *very different* from what we knew or what we thought he or she should be. Which means that we would look at the other, stop to look at him or her, ask ourselves, come close to ourselves through questioning. *Who art thou? I am* and *I become* thanks to this question. Wonder goes beyond that which is or is not suitable for us. The other never suits us simply. We would in some way have reduced the other to ourselves if he or she suited us completely. An *excess* resists: the other's existence and becoming as a place that permits union and/through resistance to assimilation or reduction to sameness.

Before and after appropriation, there is wonder. It is set apart from rejection, which expresses itself notably through contradictory positions [*par les contradictoires*]. That which precedes suitability has no opposite. In order for it to affect us, it is necessary and sufficient for it *to surprise*, to be new, *not yet assimilated or disassimilated as known*. Still awakening our passion, our appetite. Our attraction to that which is not yet (en)coded, our curiosity (but perhaps in all senses: sight, smell, hearing? etc.) vis-à-vis that which we have not yet encountered or made ours. The same as us, as myself.

Attracting me toward, wonder keeps me from taking and assimilating directly to myself. Is wonder the time that is always covered over by the *present*? The bridge, the stasis, the moment of *in-stance*? Where I am no longer in the past and not yet in the future. The point of passage between two closed worlds, two definite universes, two space-times or two others determined by their identities, two epochs, two others. A separation without a wound, awaiting or remembering, without despair or closing in on the self.

Wonder is a mourning for the self as an autarchic entity; whether this mourning is triumphant or melancholy. Wonder must be the advent or the event of the other. The beginning of a new story?

"*To wonder is united esteem or disdain according as it is at the greatness of an object or its smallness that we wonder. And we may thus esteem or despise ourselves, from which come the passions, and then the habits, of magnanimity or pride, and of humility or baseness.*" (Art. 54, p. 358; translation modified).

The object is no longer altogether unknown. It is esteemed for its size, and this size determines the quality of wonder, which is no longer pure. It has entered into the world of opposites, of contraries, and not into the opening of a new space-time. It has become energy *tied* to the dimension of the other. And not a mobilization of new energies which are still blind to their horizon, or qualities.

Moreover, here Descartes informs us about his passions: that which is great inspires esteem, magnanimity, even pride; that which is small inspires disdain, humility, even baseness. For

Descartes, there is no magnanimity vis-à-vis smallness. This can be understood as an attempt to reduce to smallness that which has disappointed our wonder, or as the inability to admire the *seed*, that which is still being born, still becoming. Can this also be interpreted as the first determining of passion in terms of the quantitative? Yet sexual difference is not reducible to the quantitative even though it is traditionally measured by such standards: by *more* or *less*.

There remains the mother, who is magnanimous toward the little one. There also remains the fact that man continually wants woman to be a mother and only a mother, loves her as if he were still very small while esteeming what is very great, possibly inventing it, becoming proud of it to the point of forgetting who he is. And his becoming.

Which interrupts the flow of time. For most passions are turned toward the future, and if they break off the path or the bridge to the past, they become lost in time. They lose themselves in an evil infinity, rather than remaining in-definite, always unlimited, taking as their limits those present in their encounter with the world, the object, the other, the God (if the subject does not create him solely to close up his world). Wandering in space and in time, the passions risk losing one of their number, the substrate of the qualities of the others, of certain others: desire. Desire would be the vectorialization of space and time, the first movement *toward*, not yet qualified. Taking as its momentum the subject's passion or the object's irresistible attraction. Sometimes more on one side, sometimes more on the other, it is not yet frozen in a predicate which would split the world in two.

In a way, wonder and desire remain the spaces of freedom between the subject and the world. The substrate of predication? Of discourse? Which often reverts to itself rather than leave the intention and the direction open to the other. Does speaking to the other, especially two-way predication, ever happen? Given our style of predication? In which the subject becomes the master of the world, of objects, of the other. In fact Descartes puts the predicate with the passions of the subject, whereby the object becomes no more than the result of the alchemy of the subject's passions. The attractive nature of the object is taken from it. Possibly, it will pass through the presentation that the other makes of it.

Except in the experience of wonder? And perhaps in *desire*, which is already secondary for Descartes. Wonder being the moment of illumination—already and still contemplative—between the subject and the world.

"Wonder is a sudden surprise of the soul which causes it to apply itself to consider with attention the objects which seem to it rare and extraordinary. It is thus primarily caused by the impression we have in the brain which represents the object as rare, and as consequently worthy of much consideration; then afterwards by the movement of the spirits, which are disposed by this impression to tend with great force towards the part of the brain where it is, in order to fortify and conserve it there; as they are also disposed by it to pass thence into the muscles which serve to retain the organs of the senses in the same situation in which they are, so that it is still maintained by them, if it is by them that it has been formed." (Art. 70, p. 362).

Descartes situates his place of inscription solely in the brain. Is wonder determined by surprise, the suddenness of the impact of rare and extraordinary objects that come to inscribe themselves in a still untouched place in the brain? Which is tender and not yet hardened by past impressions, themselves often troubled and incapable of being affected, imprinted, due to these repetitions. Wonder marks a new place, and the movement of the spirits tends toward this new place of inscription to strengthen and conserve it. Indeed: "they are also disposed by it to pass thence into the muscles which serve to retain the organs of the senses in the same situation in which they are, so that it is still maintained by them, if it is by them that it has been formed." Wonder would derive its force from the surprise and the storage of something new. It would not change anything in the heart or the blood, which are tied to good and evil, to positive or negative determinations of the thing. It would remain a purely cerebral impression and a stake in knowledge, purely a question and a striving toward the answer to the question of *who* or *what* is the object of wonder. Before even knowing whether this object corresponds or not to my body's good—which would be a matter for the heart and the blood—wonder is the appetite for knowledge of who or what awakens our appetite.

Its force derives from the fact that the appearance of something or someone new modifies the movement of spirits in an unexpected manner. This fact is specific to this passion and is also encountered in other passions because of the role that wonder plays in them. The force of the movement comes from its *beginning*. Being at the start of its trajectory, the movement has greater force than a movement that increases regularly and as such, ceaselessly risks being deflected, according to Descartes. Wonder's force also derives from the *untouched* nature of the passion's place of inscription, a characteristic that increases the amplitude of excited movements. Thus, Descartes explains, the sole of the foot is insensible to our weight when we are walking normally, but it is unbearably irritated when tickled.

"And we may say more particularly of wonder that it is useful, inasmuch as it causes us to learn and retain in our memory things of which we were formerly ignorant; for we shall only wonder at that which appears rare and extraordinary to us, and nothing can so appear excepting because we have been ignorant of it, or also because it is different from the thing we have known; for it is this difference which causes it to be called extraordinary. Now although a thing which was unknown to us, presents itself anew to our understanding or our senses, we do not for all that retain it in our memory, unless the idea which we have of it is strengthened in our brain by some passion or else by the application of our understanding which our will determines to a particular attention and reflection. And the other passions may serve to make

us remark things which seem good or evil; but we have only wonder for those which appear but seldom. We also see that those who have no natural inclination towards this passion are usually very ignorant." (Art. 75, p. 364).

For Descartes, that which is different is stimulating because it is rare and extraordinary. The beginning of the position of the subject as such still welcomes as desirable that which it does not know, that which it ignores or which remains foreign to it. *Sexual difference* could be situated there, but Descartes does not think of that. He is content with affirming that difference attracts. And stimulates memory.

Whereas the repetition of a thing undoes memory, unless it is accompanied by some passion, or our understanding makes a particular effort.

And certain passions help us notice good or bad things, but wonder alone guides us toward *rare* things. And those who have no inclination toward this passion are very ignorant. Women, according to received opinion? Do they lack this directly speculative access to the object, to the other?

But, if to wonder is a proof of intelligence and involves intellectual aptitudes, especially memory, it happens that we can wonder excessively or rashly, through a lack of intelligence. Which can take away or pervert the use of reason. And this primary passion, which has no opposite, would have to remain a passion of youth. It would be fitting to "to free ourselves of it as much as possible." For, if the will can supplement wonder by enforcing understanding, the cure for excessive wonder can only operate through the "knowledge of various matters" and the "consideration of all those which may appear the most rare and strange" (art. 76, p. 365). So as not to remain fixed on a rare object, it is appropriate to turn voluntarily toward *several* objects. So as not to be attached to one *unique* woman, is it desirable to scatter oneself among *several*?

The question of wonder and love remains. Why would these passions be separated? Do we love with the heart and blood and not through thought? Do we wonder with the head and not with the heart? Is it a matter of physiology, perhaps of Descartes's? For he describes the passions in the language of a physiologist. Would he differentiate between men and women on this point? Situating the passions at the junction of the physical and the psychological, he constructs a theory of the *ego's* affects which is close to Freud's theory of the drives. He does not differentiate the drives according to the sexes. Instead, he situates wonder as the first of the passions. Is this the passion that Freud forgot? A passion that maintains a path between physics and metaphysics, corporeal impressions and movements toward an object, whether empirical or transcendental. A primary passion and a perpetual crossroads between earth and sky, or hell, where it would be possible to rework the attraction between those who differ, especially sexually. A sort of platform or springboard for the regression of investment without engulfing, annihilation, or abolition by the other or by the world.

Could Nietzsche's *Beyond Good and Evil* signify something of a return to wonder? To a passion of pure knowledge, pure *light*? Without passing through the blood, determining good and evil, the heart and its affects, according to Descartes. Before and after acts of opposition, there would still be wonder: pure inscription, pure movement, pure memory. Even pure thought? The only *woman* whom Nietzsche can love? In a permanent form: *eternity*. The only woman with whom he wishes to have children (cf. "The Seven Seals" in *Zarathustra*). Situating woman in the place of the first and last passion. A wonder that lasts. A bridge between the instant and eternity. An attraction and return all around the unexplored, all barriers down, beyond every coast, every port. Navigating at the center of infinity, weightless. A movement lighter than the necessities of the heart, of the affect? A movement of dance or flight? Leaving the earth, its security, to navigate through fluids—marine, aerial, celestial. The passion of movement toward. Through? Which would never stop. Not even at *astonishment*, as Descartes would say. Astonishment being a kind of stupor which paralyzes. It pushes the spirits in the cavities of the brain toward the place that is wondered at, sometimes excessively, and in such a way that they stay occupied with keeping this impression and do not pass on from there into the muscles, nor are even deflected in any way from the first traces in the brain. Which means that the body stays immobile, like a statue, that of the first object there remains only the initial aspect that presented itself, and that it is not even possible to acquire new knowledge of it. An *excess of wonder* which makes one think of the shattering effects of adult love or of the permanent traces with which the child is marked without being able to be rid of them. Incapable of more wonder, of opening up to other landscapes, of moving toward new objects. Of rejuvenating one's brain, Descartes would think. Of losing one's gravity, Nietzsche would write. In which the stake is to wonder again and again without ever stopping. To steer incessantly toward the unpublished. Also to turn over everything that has already been impressed, printed, in order to liberate its impact and find its impetus on this side and beyond. The "object" of wonder or attraction remaining impossible to delimit, im-pose, identify (which is not to say lacking identity or borders): the atmosphere, the sky, the sea, the sun. That which he designates as woman-eternity, an other who is sufficiently open, cosmic, so that he can keep on moving toward her. Not the eternal feminine of images or representation(s). But a woman–mother who keeps on unfolding herself outwardly while enveloping us? And toward whom he moves, without ever getting there, without distinguishing between inside and outside. Going again and again *toward her within her*? In a movement that precedes even desire? Which protects the movement's lightness, its freedom, its continually new impulsion. Always for the first time.

Wonder is not an enveloping. It corresponds to time, to space-time before and after that which can delimit, go round, encircle. It constitutes an *opening* prior to and following that which surrounds, enlaces. It is the passion of that which is already born and not yet reenveloped in love. Of that which is touched and moves toward and within the attraction, without nostalgia for the first dwelling. Outside of repetition. It is the passion of the first encounter. And of perpetual rebirth? An affect that would subsist among all forms of others irreducible each to the other. The passion that inaugurates love and art. And thought. Is it the place of man's second birth? And of woman's? A birth into a transcendence, that of the other, still in the world of the senses ("sensible"), still physical and carnal, and already spiritual. Is it the place of incidence and junction of body and spirit, which has been covered over again and again, hardened through repetitions that hamper growth and flourishing? This would be possible only when we are faithful to the perpetual newness of the self, the other, the world. Faithful to becoming, to its virginity, its power of impulsion, without letting go the support of bodily inscription. Wonder would be the passion of the encounter between the most material and the most metaphysical, of their possible conception and fecundation one by the other. A third dimension. An intermediary. Neither the one nor the other. Which is not to say neutral or neuter. The forgotten ground of our condition between mortal and immortal, men and gods, creatures and creators. In us and among us.

The Envelope:
A Reading of Spinoza,
Ethics, "Of God"

Definitions

"By cause of itself, I understand that, whose essence involves existence; or that, whose nature cannot be conceived unless existing." (Baruch Spinoza, *Ethics*, p. 355).[1]

This definition of God could be translated as: *that which is its own place for itself*, that which turns itself inside out and thus constitutes a dwelling (for) itself. Unique and necessary. Solitary. But in itself. Sufficient. Needing no other in its reception of "space-time." Men may, perhaps, contemplate or seek to contemplate God in his place; men do not give God his place.

Which also means: that which by nature can be conceived only as existing, or: *that which provides its own envelope* by turning its essence outward, must necessarily exist. That which provides its own space-time *necessarily* exists.

Hence:

— We do not exist *necessarily* because we do not provide ourselves with our own envelopes.

[1] Page references following quotations are to Baruch (Benedict de) Spinoza, *Ethics*, Part I, "Of God," trans. W. H. White, rev. A. H. Stirling, *Great Books of the Western World*, vol. 31, *Descartes, Spinoza* (Chicago: Encyclopaedia Britannica, 1952), pp. 355–72.

— Man would thus exist more necessarily than woman because he gets his envelope from her.

Twice over:

— in or through his *necessary fetal existence,*

— in his role as *lover.* Which is contingent? Except for happiness? And becoming necessary again for procreation.

That is, he is enveloped as fetus, as lover, as father.

But

— man *receives* that envelope. By nature, it is true! And the reversal can operate just as well. Man does not provide himself with his own envelope, unless it is his nature to be conceived in woman. By essence, to be conceived in woman.

— woman would theoretically be the envelope (which she provides). But she would have no essence or existence, given that she is the potential for essence and existence: *the available place.* She would be cause for herself—and in a less contingent manner than man—if she enveloped herself, or reenveloped herself, in the envelope that she is able to "provide." The envelope that is part of her "attributes" and "affections" but which she cannot use as self cause. If she enveloped herself with what she provides, she could not but necessarily be conceived of as existing. Which, to an extent, is what happens: women's suffering arises also from the fact that man does not conceive that women do not exist. Men have such a great need that women should exist. If men are to be permitted to believe or imagine themselves as self-cause, they need to think that the envelope "belongs" to them. (Particularly following "the end of God" or "the death of God," insofar as God can be determined by an era of history in any way but through the limits to its thinking.) For men to establish this belonging—without the guarantee provided by God—it is imperative that that which provides the envelope should necessarily exist. *Therefore* the maternal-feminine exists necessarily as the cause of the self-cause of man. But not for herself. She has to exist but as an a priori condition (as Kant might say) for the space-time of the masculine subject. A cause that is never unveiled for fear that its identity might split apart and plummet down. She does not have to exist as woman because, as woman, her envelope is always *slightly open* (if man today thinks of himself as God, woman becomes, according to Meister Eckhart, an adverb or a quality of the word of God).

"*That thing is called finite in its own kind* [*in suo genere*] *which can be limited by another thing of the same nature. For example, a body is called finite, because we always conceive another which is greater. So a thought is limited by another thought; but a body is not limited by a thought, nor a thought by a body.*" (P. 355).

From which it would follow that:
— God is infinite and unlimited because nothing of the same nature exists;
— man is finite and limited
both by men of the *same nature*
and by that which is *greater*, therefore
— by the/his mother, even if he doesn't think so,
— by the/his woman, even if he doesn't think so, due to the extension of the place-envelope;
— and by *God*: but he may be so ignorant that he does not want to know that universe and thought are always greater than he is at any given moment. Does God, then, limit man by the creation and self-sufficiency of thought?

Within sexual difference, there would, it seems, be at once *finiteness and limit*, as a result of the meeting of two *bodies*, and two thoughts, and also infiniteness and unlimitedness if "God" intervenes.

If there are not *two* bodies and *two* thoughts, according to Spinoza, an evil infinite may occur: with the thought of the one limiting the body of the other and vice versa. There is no longer finiteness, or limits, or access to the infinite. At best, is matter made into form by the act? Which would virtually happen once, then once more, plus one, plus one, plus one. . . . A multiplicity of feminine formations that have access neither to the finite nor to the infinite.

If man and woman are both body and thought, they provide each other with finiteness, limit, and the possibility of access to the divine through the development of envelopes. Greater and greater envelopes, vaster and vaster horizons, but above all envelopes that are qualitatively more and more necessary and different. But always *overflowing*: with the female one becoming a cause of the other by providing him with self-cause. The setup must always be open for this to occur. It must also afford a *qualitative* difference. Essence must never be completely realized in existence—as Spinoza might say? Perhaps, for men, the movement is made in reverse? It is through existence that they can discover essence? Men would not unfold their essence into existence but by virtue of existence would, perhaps, successfully constitute an essence.

Within sexual difference, therefore, *finiteness*, *limit*, and *progression* are needed: and this requires two bodies, two thoughts, a relation between the two and the conception of a wider perspective.

Clearly, for Spinoza, a body is not limited by a thought or a thought by a body. The two remain "parallel" and never intersect. The question of sexual difference, a question to be thought out particularly after and with the "death of God" and the period of the ontic-ontological difference, requires a reconsideration of the split between body and thought. The whole historic or historial analysis of philosophy shows that being has yet to be referred to in terms of body or flesh (as Heidegger notes in "Logos," his seminar on Heraclitus).[2] Thought and body have

---

[2] Martin Heidegger, "Logos (Heraclitus, Fragment B 50)," in *Early Greek Thinking: The Dawn of Western Philosophy*, trans. David F. Krell and Frank A. Capuzzi (New York: Harper and Row, 1975), pp. 59–78.

remained separate. And this leads, on the social and cultural level, to important empirical and transcendental effects: with *discourse* and *thought* being the privileges of a *male* producer. And that remains the "norm." Even today, bodily tasks remain the obligation or the duty of a female subject. The break between the two produces rootless and insane thinking as well as bodies (women and children) that are heavy and slightly "moronic" because they lack language.

Does the act of love then mean that thinking about the body receives an infusion of flesh? Clearly, to take may be to give. And this is already a way out of parallelism. The two sexes would penetrate each other by means of theft or a rape, a more or less mechanical encounter whose goal would be to produce a child. To produce a body? Or just body? As long as our thinking is unable to limit the body, or vice versa, no sex act is possible. Nor any thought, any imaginary or symbolic of the flesh. The empirical and the transcendental have split apart (just like the roles fulfilled by man and woman?) and the body falls on one side, language on the other.

"By substance, I understand that which is in itself and is conceived through itself; in other words, that, the conception of which does not need the conception of another thing from which it must be formed." (P. 355).

Here Spinoza is talking about God. Only God is in himself, conceived by himself; needing the concept of no other thing in order to be formed. Only God generates his existence out of his essence; which means also that he engenders himself in the form of concepts without having need of concepts different from himself in order to be formed.

God alone is *in self, by self* [*en soi, par soi*], in an autodetermination that is linked to the in-itself [*en-soi*]. Does *in self by self* amount to a definition of place that develops itself? Does *in self conceived by self* mean: capable of providing and limiting its place? Never to be determined and limited by anything but self. Itself autoaffecting itself, potentially, as in the middle-passive, but never passively affected by anything else. Not knowing

[*87*]

passivity. Never power [*puissance*], body-extension, available to suffer the action of an other than self.

That said, if this definition can be applied to God alone, the definition is defined, and God is defined, by man and not by God himself. Therefore God determines himself conceptually out of man. He does not proffer his own conception, except through the mouth of man. Obviously, in certain traditions and at certain periods, God designates himself: in words, in the texts of the law, through incarnation in different modes. But, in most cases, it is man who names in the form of conceptions, and who situates God in that space as far as the generation of conception goes.

It also seems that *Man* conceives himself without anyone else, except God, forming his conception. But the relation of man to God, of God to man, often seems circular: man defines God who in turn determines man.

This would not be the case for *woman*, who would correspond to no conception. Who, as the Greeks saw it, lacks fixed form and idea, and lacks above all a conception that she provides for herself. As matter, or extension for the concept, she would have no conception at her disposal, would be unable to conceive herself or conceive the other, and, theoretically, she would need to pass through man in order to have a relation, for herself, to man, to the world, and to God. If indeed she is capable of any of this.

Axioms

> "*Everything which is, is either in itself or in another.*" (P. 355).
> Being is determined by the place that envelops it:
> — either the envelope is the essence of the existing thing or
>   of existence (see "Of God," Definitions, I). That which
>   is, is *in self.*
> — or else that which is, is *in something other*, depends on the
>   existence of something other: is not cause of self.

[*88*]

The Envelope

That which is, is determined by that in which it is contained—by that which envelops it, envelops its existence.

"*That which cannot be conceived* through *another must be conceived* through *itself.*" (P. 355).

Refer to the commentary on the Definitions, III. Definition of substance.

Not to be *in* self means being in something other. This is still the problem of place, of the need to receive place (unless one is God), as a result of the passage from middle-passive to passive, from auto-affection to hetero-affection, from auto-determination, auto-engendering, to determination, creation, even pro-creation by someone other. From the necessary circularity and conceptional self-sufficiency of God to the difference of that which can be conceived *by*, or even *in*, something other.

"*From a given determinate cause an effect necessarily follows; and, on the other hand, if no determinate cause be given, it is impossible that an effect can follow.*" (P. 355).

Everything takes place in a chain of causalities, in a genealogical sequence of *there is*'s. There has to be a cause that is already given, already existing, if there is to be an effect, a necessary effect. But does the cause that is already given result from an essence that is not given as such? Not in the works of Spinoza? Where God and nature are coessentials?

What relation is there between the given cause and the revealed cause? The *data*, the *there is*, the problem of the neuter case, and the fact God will be referred to in the neuter as *indeterminatum, non datum*.

But, to return to my hypothesis, if the feminine does not manifest itself as cause, it can engender no effects. And yet the maternal-feminine is also *cause of causes*. Does that mean that it too is an *indeterminatum* in its way? Insofar as it always lies behind the *data*. Behind that which is already determined in the chain of causalities. Or else: the chain of causalities on the female side

[89]

remains unrevealed. Still to be unveiled. The maternal-feminine would unfold, offer, manifest itself in the form of *data* that are not determined, not given *as such*. No effects would thereby ensue. And all this would remain possible for lack of any thought about the body and the flesh. For lack of a reciprocal determination of the one by the other, as opposed to the parallelism that prevents the maternal-feminine from being inscribed in duration as causes and effects. This in fact leaves the masculine *lost* in the chain of causalities as far as the male body, the male flesh, is concerned, as well as their relations to conception, the cause of self, except by means of the absolute causality that is God.

As for the feminine, this absence of inscription of its causes and effects in the chain of causalities leads, for example, to Aristotle's notion that woman is engendered as if by *accident*. A genetic aberration. An illness. A monstrosity. Or again, the notion that the child is engendered from the male seed alone. The female seed would not be necessary. It is not a cause and, if anything, *impedes* the possibility of generation. (See this strange quotation, among many others, from Aristotle, who was, nevertheless, a doctor: "Here is an indication that the female does not discharge semen of the same kind as the male, and that the offspring is not formed from a mixture of two semens, as some allege. Very often the female conceives although she has derived no pleasure from the act of coitus; and, on the contrary side, when the female derives as much pleasure as the male, and they both keep the same pace, the female does not bear—unless there is a proper amount of menstrual fluid [as it is called] present.")[3]

The female, it seems, is pure disposable "matter." Pure receptacle that does not stay still. Not even a place, then? Always belonging to a threatening primitive chaos. That even God should never approach. For fear he may suffer its obscure effects? Could the female be effect(s) without cause? Necessary

---

[3] *Aristotle: Generation of Animals*, trans. A. L. Peck (Cambridge: Harvard University Press, 1963), pp. 97–98.

cause. Raised as an issue only as the *accidental* cause of man? A genetic mistake. Or a divine whim? With God giving birth to the woman out of the body of the man.

"The knowledge [cognitio] of an effect depends upon and involves knowledge of the cause." (P. 355).

Does knowledge of an effect envelop knowledge of the cause by a retroactive process? Which, however, by enveloping, hides the knowledge, veils it, and perhaps gives birth to it by a round-about or return route to generation?

When knowledge of the effect envelops that of the cause, this can evoke the maternal-feminine, even in its most physical effects of generation as it doubles back on the "masculine" and its thought, and overwhelms it. Because it is not thought of as a cause, does the maternal-feminine mask cause? Overwhelm it with a veil (that of the illusion of flesh? or the veil of Maya?). Hide it? We shall need to decipher, work through, interpret the knowledge of *effects* in order to achieve knowledge of *causes*. Is this a reverse knowledge? Why is it that the *data* are not already thought of as effects? Why is *cause* already *caused*? Because it comes from God? With cause already being effect, but of God. We can agree that there should be no effects without cause, but cause is already a given effect, or even an effect of an effect. To the genealogy of causes corresponds a hierarchy of effects. Two parallel chains which do not always cross and yet mutually determine each other, in particular as they roll and unroll reciprocally. That which is self-cause is an envelope for itself, which develops into existence(s), but is enveloped by our knowledge of its effects. As it reveals its existence to us, we envelop-veil it with the knowledge of its effects, on the basis of which we seek knowledge of its cause(s).

Does knowledge of the effect envelop knowledge of the cause? The effect overwhelms the cause from the point of view of knowledge. A double movement in "theology," moving up and down. Essence envelops existence if there is *cause of self*, knowledge of the effect envelops that of the cause if there is no cause of self. If I start with the creatures, I move up the chain of effects (until, perhaps, I reach an uncreated cause whose knowledge, or ultimate cause, escapes us?); if I start with God, I move down the chain of causes, on the basis of a *causa sui*.

There are no effects without an already given cause. And this is linked to the question of *miracles* for Spinoza. There might be effects without *data*: inexplicable, "miraculous" effects. Before deciding for a "miracle," Spinoza notes our inability to perceive the extension of the chain of causalities and, in particular, our inability to analyze the relation of contingency to necessity. A belief in "miracle" or in "chance" is often a result of weakness or narrowness in the field of conception.[4]

"*Those things which have nothing mutually in common with one another cannot through one another be mutually understood, that is to say, the conception of the one does not involve the conception of the other.*" (P. 355).

Conception means taking hold of, perceiving, and conceiving an available matter or power. Conception is more active than perception; or, more exactly, conception designates the active pole of the mind, and perception designates the passive pole. Whence the fact that, traditionally, the feminine, insofar as it has access to mind, remains in perception, while the conception is the privilege of the masculine.

I am often asked this question: if sexual difference exists, what path can there still be between man and woman? Which amounts to saying that in the past relations between men and women were not determined by sex. In Spinoza's terms, this is to assume that woman cannot conceive. Or else that man can't? (but that cannot be so, since Spinoza is conceiving his system . . .).

If sexual difference exists, does that mean that man and

---

[4] See, for example, Spinoza, *Ethics*, proposition 33, scholium 1 (p. 367): "But a thing cannot be called contingent unless with reference to a deficiency in our knowledge."

woman hold nothing in common? There is at the very least the child as an effect, as we know. In our thinking, clearly, the child is still thought of as an effect of man's, of the male seed, even if biology has established that this is not so. Our thinking still thinks of the ovum as passive, of the female body as passivity, of woman as remaining in the domain of perception, or even at times of the perceived.

What would man and woman have in common? Both conception and perception. *Both*. And without any hierarchy between the two. Both would have the capacity to perceive and conceive. *To suffer and to be active*. To suffer the self and to understand the self. To receive the self and to envelop the self. Becoming more open because of the freedom of each, male and female. Since freedom and necessity are correlated. With each giving the other necessity and freedom. In self, for self, and for the other.

If I exist, that would mean that I correspond to a necessity. Therefore that I should be free. For this to become so, the concept of the masculine would have to cease to envelop that of the feminine, since the feminine has no necessity if it is uniquely an effect of and for the masculine.

Between man and woman, whatever the differences may be and despite the fact that the concept of the one, male or female, cannot envelop that of the other, certain bridges can be built, through two approaches:

— that of generation,
— that of God.

But, historically, in Genesis, the feminine has no conception. She is figured as being born from man's envelope, with God as midwife. Whereas woman envelops man before his birth. Could it be that God is he who intervenes so that there should be a *reciprocal limitation* of envelopes for both? Which is why it is necessary to go through the question of God every time the sexual act comes under consideration.

The openings in the envelopes between men and women should always be mediated by God. Faithless to God, man lays down the law for woman, imprisons her in his conception(s), or at least in accordance with his conceptions instead of covering her only for God, while awaiting God. Woman, who enveloped man before birth, until he could live outside her, finds herself encircled by a language, by places that she cannot conceive of, and from which she cannot escape.

It's nothing new for man to want to be both man and woman: he has always had pretensions of turning the envelope inside out. But by willing to be master of everything, he becomes the slave both of discourse and of mother nature.

III

Love of Same,
Love of Other

Love of Same, Substrate for All Others

Love of same may be understood as undifferentiated attraction to the archaic, as love of that which does not and will not know itself as different. Unless we rethink the whole history of philosophy, everything that history has proposed or imposed upon us as frames for thought and affect. Which would include the origin of its potency [*puissance*], specifically as that relates to the fluids that it never speaks of (that are always left *between* the lines of what is said, perhaps to ensure its cohesion?).

Love of same is love for that which primevally and necessarily has conceived, given birth, nourished, warmed.

Love of same is love of indifferentiation from the earth-mother, the first living dwelling place.

Love of same is love of the ontic that will make matter for the transcendent other. The ontic-ontological split would merely be an effect of *forgetting*: the result of a jump between the body or the flesh of that which is and that which wishes to be.

Love of Other would be a love of same that does not recognize itself as such. Whence the resistance that it sets up to interpretation. The Other can exist only if it can draw on the well of sameness for its matter, for the texture of its horizon, the emergence of its beyond-world. If this were not so, that Other would be so other that we could in no way conceive it. But the Other does not wish to—or perhaps cannot?—interpret its relationship to sameness because it thereby loses its substance.

This same of the Other can be interpreted, can be spoken, as matter for being [*étant*] as well as for discourse, and as that which constitutes the tissue of and in ontology.

This same of the Other is matter, flux, interstices, blanks . . . all still available, in stock, already forgotten

This sameness is matter and place, universe and things, container and contained, contents and envelope, waters and firmament. (In the beginning, says Genesis, God divided the waters and made the firmament between the waters: those under and those above the firmament.)

It is this sameness that constitutes the subject as a living being but that man has not begun to think: his body.[1]

This sameness, womblike and maternal, serves forever and *for free*, unknown, forgotten.

This sameness is not abyss; it neither devours nor engulfs. It is an availability so available that for one who lives for utility, for mastery, the cash nexus, debt, this assumption of availability— which precedes any position that can be discerned—arouses anxiety and hence efforts to name and designate causes.

This sameness is the maternal-feminine which has been assimilated before any perception of difference. The red blood, the lymph, for every body, every discourse, every creation, every making of a world. "Although twice forgotten, she remains a dusky background, a sleep of oblivion out of which he erects

---

[1] See what Martin Heidegger says in this regard in his seminar on Heraclitus, "Logos (Heraclitus, Fragment B 50)," in *Early Greek Thinking: The Dawn of Western Philosophy*, trans. David F. Krell and Frank A. Capuzzi (New York: Harper and Row, 1975), pp. 59–78.

himself, and an imperceptible transparence for the entry into presence."[2]

It is because this same, and the Other's relation to it, is priceless that it unquestionably poses the greatest danger we face today.

Love of the Same Other

No love for that which is the same as me, but placed and maintained outside myself in its difference, can take place without

— an interpretation of the love of sameness: a still undifferentiated maternal-feminine, substrate for any possible determination of identity;

— a point of view that would emerge from or transcend that ancient relationship;

— a horizon of sexual difference.

Three conditions that are really one.

Love of Same among Men or in the Masculine

At the dawn of our culture, access to differentiation occurs through the affirmation of the body. The Greek takes hold of himself as one who is separated from infinite nature by his bodily being. Athletic prowess and valor are the qualities essential for the Homeric hero. Through strength and skill in combat he learns to take hold of himself, place himself.

But man will forget this. The world, or worlds, that he constructs will close over him so tightly that reaching something

2 See Luce Irigaray, *L'Oubli de l'air, chez Martin Heidegger* (Paris: Minuit, 1983), in which this relation to sameness is a major issue.

outside him becomes difficult for him. He does not even remember the fact that his body is the threshold, the portal for the
construction of his universe, or universes. He exists in his nostalgia for a return to the ONE WHOLE; his desire to go back
toward and into the originary womb.

Alone, he cannot undertake this journey home. It is impossible or taboo unless he is sure of a foundation within which there
is place.

The affirmation of the body, and the love of the body, which
are still spoken of in the Homeric epic, at the beginning of
philosophy, will finally be forgotten in the metaphysical edifice.
They will appear only in technical fields that are subordinate to
the first philosophy: in medicine, for example.

On the other hand, love of sameness becomes that which
permits the erection of space-time or space-times, as well as the
constitution of a customarily autarchic discourse which opens
up only toward a dialogue-monologue with God.

Love of sameness is transformed, transmuted into an architecture of world or worlds, into a system of symbolic and mercan-
tile exchanges. It becomes fabrication and creation of tools and
products. Instead of germination, birth, and growth in accordance with natural economy, man substitutes the instrument
and the product. Harvests become a mere outcome of agricul-
ture, as products do of industry. Man cultivates nature and manages its conservation, but often at the price of birth and growth.
The cultivation of nature becomes exploitation, which risks destroying the vitality of the soil and the fertility of the great
cosmic rhythms. This is the danger we incur when we forget
what we have received from the body, our debt toward that
which gives and renews life. When we forget our gratitude toward the living being that man is at every instant.

The love of sameness among men often means a love within
sameness, which cannot posit itself as such without the
maternal-natural-material. It represents the love of a production
by assimilation and mediation of the female or females. It often

constitutes a kind of ontology of the anal[3] or else a triumph of the absorption of the other into the self in the intestine.[4] Often in these constitutions, love is played out in terms of the product, and the strength which love manifests is owed in particular to the tool.

This production which we see in men (even when it's a question of their bodies) is not unrelated to the fecal object and the ambiguous relationship to blood it sets up by wanting to be nobler than blood while in fact being merely its waste product or remainder, likely to bring pollution. This is often the way with the creations of men. Analogous (?) to the way men feel or imagine themselves? Things produced outside them, not engendered, within them, by a patient labor of the blood?

Their love is teleological. It aims for a target outside them. It moves toward the outside and to the constitution, on the outside, within that which is outside themselves, of a home. Outside the self, the tension, the intention, aims for a dwelling, a thing, a production. Which also serves men as third part and stake.

Love of Self among Women and in the Feminine

The love of self among women, in the feminine, is very hard to establish. Traditionally, it is left in the undifferentiation of the mother-daughter relationship. And this relationship has to be given up, Freud tells us, if the woman is to enter into desire for the man-father.[5] A dimension that must be denied in word and

---

[3] See what Maurice Merleau-Ponty has to say on this issue in the work notes at the end of the collection *The Visible and the Invisible*, trans. Alphonso Lingis (Evanston: Northwestern University Press, 1968), pp. 165–275.

[4] See G. W. F. Hegel, *The Phenomenology of Mind*, trans. J. B. Baillie (New York: Harper Torchbooks, 1967), pp. 464–82, and my own reading, "The Eternal Irony of the Community," in *Speculum of the Other Woman* (Ithaca: Cornell University Press, 1985), pp. 214–26.

[5] See my interpretation of this in "The Blind Spot of an Old Dream of Symmetry," in *Speculum of the Other Woman*, pp. 11–129.

act if the good health of family and city is to be ensured, Hegel wrote.[6] Does this mean that love of the mother among women can and may be practiced only through *substitution*? By a taking the place of? Which is unconsciously colored by hate?

Since the mother has a unique place, to become a mother would supposedly be to occupy that place, without having any relationship to the mother in that place. The economy, here, would be *either the one woman or the other,* either her or I-me. This rivalry in regard to place and the maternal functions (the only functions for women that are valued in the West) is ruled by man's relation to the maternal and by the lack of a female identity. If we are to be desired and loved by men, we must abandon our mothers, substitute for them, eliminate them in order to be *same.* All of which destroys the possibility of a love between mother and daughter. The two become at once accomplices and rivals in order to move into the single possible position in the desire of man.

This competition equally paralyzes love among sister-women. Because they strive to achieve the post of *the unique one: the mother of mothers,* one might say. During this polemic as to who will be the winner in the maternal power stakes, women perpetuate the privilege accorded to the attraction of son for mother, mother for son. The most perfect configuration love can take, writes Freud. Prototype of the relation of the god incarnate in the feminine. This is what is essentially at stake in incest, in its strength, in the taboos surrounding it, its repression as a foundation for our culture.

One configuration remains in latency, in abeyance: that of *love among women.* A configuration that constitutes a substrate that is sometimes mute, sometimes a disturbing force in our culture. A

[6] See Hegel, "The Ethical World," in *The Phenomenology of Mind,* and my reading of it, "The Eternal Irony of the Community," in *Speculum of the Other Woman.*

very live substrate whose outlines, shapes, are yet blurred, chaotic, or confused.

Traditionally, therefore, this love among women has been a matter of rivalry with:

— the real mother,

— an all-powerful prototype of maternity,

— the desire of man: of father, son, brother.

This involves *quantitative estimates* of love that ceaselessly interrupt love's attraction and development. When we hear women talking to each other, we tend to hear expressions like the following:

— like you;

— me too;

— me more (or me less).

Such nagging calculations (which may be unconscious or preconscious) paralyze the fluidity of affect. We harden, borrow, situate ourselves on the edges of the other in order to "exist." As proofs of love, these comparatives eliminate the possibility of a place among women. We prize one another by standards that are not our own and which occupy, without inhabiting, the potential place of our identity. These statements bear witness to affects which are still childish or which fail to survive the death struggle of a narcissism that is always put off: to infinity or else to the hands of a third party as judge.

One of the remarks you often hear one woman say to another woman who is a little better situated in her identity is: *just like everyone else.* Here we have no proof of love, but a judgmental statement that prevents the woman from standing out from an undifferentiated grouping, from a sort of primitive community of women, unconscious utopias or atopias that some women exploit at times to prevent one of their number from affirming her identity.

Without realizing it, or willing it, in most cases, women constitute the most terrible instrument of their own oppression: they destroy anything that emerges from their undifferentiated condition and thus become agents of their own annihilation, their reduction to a sameness that is not *their own*. A kind of magma, of "night in which all the cats are gray," from which man, or humanity, extracts for free what he needs for food, lodging, and survival.

These *like you, me too, me more (or less), just like everyone else* kinds of remarks have little to do with a loving ethics. They are trace-symptoms of the *polemos*[7] among women. There is no *with you* in this economy. But there may be a fusional state out of which nothing emerges or should emerge, or else a blind competition to occupy a place or space that is ill-defined but which arouses attraction, envy, passion. It is still not another woman who is loved but merely the *place* she occupies, that she creates, and that must be taken away from her, rather than respected.

This tends to be the way with passions among women. We have to move against the current of history for things to be any different. Which does happen. And constitutes one of the most essential places for an ethics of the passions: *no love of other without love of same.*

This love of same is difficult to establish among women also because what women provide is not symbolized as a manufactured object, because it remains like a raw material that is freely available and which is hard to imagine. At least as long as there is any of it left.

A symbolism has to be created among women if love among them is to take place. Right now in fact, such a love is possible only among women who are able to talk to each other. Lacking this interval *of exchange*, whether of words or deeds, women's passions work on an animal or vegetal level, in a rather cruel manner. Why, on what grounds, does society, does the commu-

[7] (Although *polemos* is usually translated as "war," Irigaray does not seem to have a standard meaning in mind. Like *polemic* in English, several French words having to do with verbal debates stem from this word. The reader is advised to attend to the contexts in which Irigaray uses *polemos*.—Tr.)

nity, have an interest in maintaining women's silence? In order to perpetuate all the existing norms of the society and the culture which also depend on separating women from each other.

If women are to establish or make possible a love among us, or a love for the feminine among us, women need to double and play what we are twice over, lovingly. Whether it be
— love for the *nourishing envelope*, both inner and outer, for its skins and its mucous membranes;
— love of the *body*: both of that body we give and of that body we give each other back in return.
Women must love one another both as mothers, with a maternal love, and as daughters, with a filial love. *Both of them*. In a female whole that, furthermore, is not closed off. Constituting, perhaps, both of them in one female whole that is not closed up, the sign of *infinity*? Achieving, through their relations with each other, a path into infinity that is always open, *in-finite*.

The topology of the subject as it has been defined by certain theoreticians of psychoanalysis (such as Jacques Lacan) and certain logicians places this symbolizing soil or substrate which the feminine constitutes at the service of the (male) subject. As the subject functions according to the schema of a Möbius strip, moving from inside to outside, from outside to inside, without changing edges, it would *close off* the cycle of love between mother and daughter, among women. By making an enclosure of a topology or morphology that must remain open, the subject would repress it, constitute it as substrate, no longer free and fertile in its own becoming but peopled with monsters that have to be locked away. Thus, in most cases, the maternal-feminine is the source of fear or repugnance for the subject who has buried the feminine deep in the earth. Paralyzing her movements, her economy, her culture, her love or loves.
Women, in a way quite different from that of the traditional subject of discourse (which is called neuter but in fact histori-

An Ethics of Sexual Difference

cally has been masculine), move from the greater to the smaller, traversing an infinite number of dimensions of the universe without need of a fixed point underfoot. From the most child-like to the most adult of the generation, from the most elementary to the most divine, women move around and about without changing matter or universe, providing that no one, man or woman, holds them down in one place, one space.

Women run these courses while remaining both in motion and stable. Both. Their movement is virtually continued in place. Still and moving, they do not exercise their strength over a third party. Their power does not move according to the teleology of the construction of a world, of worlds, and does not have a view to *going toward*. Women move almost without moving. They generate without there being any neat distinction, any eternal perception of what comes before and what after. The turn, or return, of genealogy is repeated indefinitely in woman/women, among women, like a ceaseless voyage.

What is sometimes difficult for women is to provide themselves with a *periphery*, a circumference, a world, a home. According to a cycle that overwhelms systems of taking-discarding, or taking-leaving, but which is able to operate and be operated on the periphery. *At a distance*, should one say? Energy that might be saved, used in self-engendering, in creating one's own horizon, in its imaginary, artistic, and cultural dimensions. Its divine dimensions also. In many traditions, the god is engendered by means of a woman, means that are not simply the practical ones of procreation. Women take part in the divine becoming, in the engendering of "God." But that mediation is often forgotten. Women serve the apparition of the god but do not appear themselves as *divine*. As *mothers* of God, as *servants* of the Lord, yes. As consorts of the god, as incarnations of the divinity, no.

In fact women *have* no soul. Is this because women are interiority and also exteriority? Often they lack the power to experience the inward and the outward, more particularly because they live their lives as a *threshold* that ensures passage between the two.

If this threshold (this ground that is no ground) is ever to be lived *for women's benefit,* they need language, some language [*le langage, du langage*]. This linguistic home that man has managed to substitute even for his dwelling in a body, whether his own body or another's, has used women as construction material, but (therefore?) it is not available to her.

The language system, or system of languages, doubled or accompanied by epistemological formalism and formal logic, takes from women and excludes them from the threshold of living in the word. Bars women from the to-and-fro of words, from the traversal of words that would allow them both to get out of and to return to their own homes To "take off" from their bodies, give themselves a territory, an environment, and invite the other to some possible share or passage.

Because women have no language sexed as female, they are used in the elaboration of a so-called neuter language where in fact they are deprived of speech. And this makes it hard for a woman to achieve a *for-itself,* and to construct a place between the *in-itself* and the *for-itself.* In the terms of the Hegelian dialectic, this situation might be analyzed as the female remaining in the *plant* world without any chance of creating an *animal* territory for herself. This female world would be paralyzed in its ethical development. The women's way of achieving ethical action is forbidden them by the laws of the city.[8] Antigone is thrust out of the city, "extradited" from the city-state, refused a home and the most elementary domestic rituals (serving the dead, the gods, preparing food), forbidden to speak, to marry, to bear children. She is walled up in a cave on the border of the world of citizens; she may neither leave nor enter her home. Every act is forbidden her. All that she can do is to carry out the

[8] See Hegel, "The Ethical World," in *The Phenomenology of Mind.*

deed that king and state dare not do openly but which they collude in, to the point of performing the burial: she can kill herself. She has barely been allowed a little air, a crack in the rock to permit breath. She herself sacrifices this vestige of plant life, which is all that has been left to her. Like a plant buried in a stone cave which can only live if it manages to get out of its tomb, rise up into the light. This is impossible for Antigone, given her human dimensions. Physically, she is too human to flee, to escape this prison. But, even though Antigone needs to escape the stone, she also has to shake off the control, the empire of *a* law if she is to move within herself and within the universe as if in a living home. It is crucial she be given her share of life, blood, air, water, fire, not just that she be present to offer worship to something already dead: whether individuals or laws. Antigone's actions must not be dismissed as respect for her father's family, fear of the gods of the underworld, or obedience to order in a state that forbids her any ethical action of her own.

If we are not to relive Antigone's fate, the world of women must successfully create an ethical order and establish the conditions necessary for women's action. This world of female ethics would continue to have two vertical and horizontal dimensions:
— daughter-to-mother, mother-to-daughter;
— among women, or among "sisters."

In some way, the vertical dimension is always being taken away from female becoming. The bond between mother and daughter, daughter and mother, has to be broken for the daughter to become a woman. Female genealogy has to be suppressed, on behalf of the son-Father relationship, and the idealization of the father and husband as patriarchs. But without a vertical dimension (since verticality has always been confused with erection), a loving ethical order cannot take place among women. Within themselves, among themselves, women need both of these dimensions (even squared . . .) if they are to act ethically, either to achieve an *in-itself for-itself*, a move out of the plant life into the animal, or to organize their "animal" territoriality into a "state" or people with its own symbols, laws, and gods.

Because this horizon has still to be built, women cannot remain merely a horizontality, ground for the male erection. Women must construct a *world* in all its and their dimensions. A universe, not merely *for the other*, as they have been asked to do in the past: as keepers of home and children, mothers, in the name of the property, the laws, the rights, and obligations of the other's State.

A world for women. Something that at the same time has never existed and which is already present, although repressed, latent, potential. Eternal mediators for the incarnation of the body and the world of man, women seem never to have produced the singularity of their own body and world. The originality of a sameness that would relate to incarnation. Before and after the advent into the light of day. Before and after the movement outward into the brightness of the outside of the body, of the inside of a world. This *sameness*, quite apart from everything that can be said about it from the outside, has a way of relating to its appearance which cannot be equated with that of the masculine world, as a result of the way it lives in *mucous*.

The mucous, in fact, is experienced from within. In the prenatal and loving night known by both sexes. But it is far more important in setting up the intimacy of bodily perception and its threshold for women. Does the mucous perhaps take the place of the soul for women? But of a soul that is never spoken? Alien to everything yet said of the soul as such? Since the mucous has no permanence, even though it is the "tissue" for the development of duration. The condition of possibility for the extension of time? But only insofar as as it is made available to and for a masculine subject that erects itself out of the mucous. And which believes it is based on substances, on something solid. All of which requires the mucous to blur in its potency and its act (in its potentially autonomous *hypokeimenon?*)[9] and to serve merely as a means for the elaboration of the substantial, the essential.

However, it is possible that the mucous corresponds to something that needs to be thought through today. For different reasons and imperatives:

— Any thinking of or about the female has to think through the mucous.

— No thinking about sexual difference that would not be traditionally hierarchical is possible without thinking through the mucous.

— In its extension, in its property of expansion, does the mucous not correspond to what Heidegger designates as the crucial issue our generation has to think through?[10]

— On the other hand, the fact that the mucous has been taken out of the order of numbers might indicate the place of its threshold, its limit, its relation to the divine, which has yet to be thought out.

— At issue would be a kind of divinity with whom one might be welcoming, festive, specifically because the God that Nietzsche talked about is dead. In other words, because the mucous has a special touch and properties, it would stand in the way of the transcendence of a God that was alien to the flesh, a God of immutable, stable truth. On the contrary, the mucous would summon the god to return or to come in a new incarnation, a new parousia.

— Because the mucous represents perhaps something that would accomplish or reverse dialectic. The transparence of the concept would be countered by the non-

[9] (*Hypokeimenon* is "that which underlies being," "prime matter," or "the basis."—Tr.)
[10] See Martin Heidegger, "The Fundamental Question for Metaphysics," in *An Introduction to Metaphysics*, trans. Ralph Manheim (New Haven: Yale University Press, 1959), pp. 1–51.

transparence, the *other* transparence of the mucous. Never merely something available, never merely a material ready for some hand or some tool to use to construct a piece of work. And equally something that cannot possibly be denied. That always leaves a trace behind: nostalgia for a return to the womb, a wound seeking a place deeper than the skin, a quest for a way into or out of the self and the other, for a meeting with the other who is never situated or expected. Impossible to suppress or forget entirely, without trace, it is only in an *act* that the mucous perceives and loves itself without thesis, without position outside itself. The potency achieves "its" act which is never set in a finished piece of work. But which is always *half open*. Never amounts simply to consumption. To producing some child. While serving love, respiration, song, without ever taking hold of itself as such. This explains the insatiability of one who can find no rhythm in the act. The anxiety of the chasm, of the abyss, equally, on the part of the man who neither welcomes nor finds a rhythm for the act of love. This failure to embrace the mucous leads to the squandering of its abundance, the exploitation of its availability, its joyfulness, its flesh, or to the abandonment and repetition of its gesture or gestures of love, which become broken and jerky, instead of progressive and inscribed in duration.

Love of the Other

If we are to have a sense of the other that is not projective or selfish, we have to attain an intuition of the infinite:
— either the intuition of a god or divine principle aiding in the birth of the other without pressuring it with our own desire,

— or the intuition of a subject that, at each point in the present, remains unfinished and open to a becoming of the other that is neither simply passive nor simply active.

If we fail to turn toward the other in this way, hatred becomes the *apeiron*, the dimension of the un-finished or of the Infinite [*de l'in-fini ou Infini*]. With this dimension being transmuted by and into a theory or a set of concepts which are not worked out on the basis of love of the other. As is virtually the norm in our tradition.

Consequently, the *Other* often stands in our tradition for *product of a hatred for the other*. Not intended to be open to interpretation. The Other constitutes a love of sameness that has no recognition of itself as such and is raised to the dimension of a transcendent that ensures and guards the whole world entity. In this way God functions as the keystone of language, of sign and symbol systems.

God is beyond this world, but supposedly he already ensures its coherence here and now. Fluid, an interstitial flux, that cements the unity of everything and allows us to believe that the love of sameness has been overcome, whereas in fact that love has been raised to an incalculable power and swallows up the love of the other—the maternal-feminine other—which has been assimilated to sameness. Equally annihilated by sameness is the nonthetic love of self, which still finds no representation.

This Other, placed as keystone to the whole order of language, of semantic architecture, has for centuries been scrupulously protected by the word of men, sometimes only by that of the clerics, in a kind of inescapable circularity or tautology: in order to protect that which or He Who offered them protection.

Nietzsche used to say that we would continue to believe in God as long as we believed in grammar. Yet even, or perhaps particularly after the fall of a certain God, discourse still defends its untouchable status. To say that discourse has a *sex*, especially in its syntax, is to question the last bastion of semantic order. It amounts to taking issue with the God of men in his most traditional form. Even if language is emptied of meaning—or per-haps the more it is emptied of meaning?—respect for its techni-cal architecture must remain intact. Discourse would be the erection of the *totem* and the *taboo* of the world of man.

And the more man strives to analyze the world, the universe, himself, the more he seems to resist *upsetting the foundations of discourse*. His analysis would serve only to confirm and double discourse's immutability. From the start, discourse would be for man that other of nature, that mother, that nature-womb, with-in which he lived, survived, and risked being lost. The discourse that had been intended as his tool for breaking ground and cultivating the world changed into an intangible, sacred horizon for him. That which is most his own and yet most alien to him? His home within the universe. And, inside that tentacular tech-nical machine that man has made, a machine that threatens him today, not only in stark reality but also by assimilation to his fantasies and the nightmares he has of a devouring mother, man seems to cling ever tighter to that semblance of familiarity he finds in both his everyday and his scientific discourse. As if that technical universe and that language were not his creation, which, because of its failure to preserve the other, fails to pre-serve him too. The work of his hand, in which he cannot even recognize himself, in which he has drowned the other, now threatens to drown him in turn. He has all the animist fears of a child in the face of nature. He is afraid to touch his machine in case it is activated by his approach, as if it were a mechanism owed respect because of its transcendence. Language, in all its shapes and sizes, would dimly represent for man the all-powerful and ever-unknown mother as well as the transcendent God. *Both*. Man cannot or will not recognize or reinterpret in his symbols this duality in his technical productions

The most obvious symbol, that closest to hand and also most easily forgotten, is the *living symbol* of sexual difference. But theory would claim that this symbolizes only itself. And women would serve only as a potential symbol to be exchanged by men, by peoples, and would never achieve symbolism or be able to use symbols.[11] Does the symbol constituted by sexual difference implacably split into two? The female would fall into the category of fallow land, matter to be made into a product, or currency symbol, mother or virgin without any identity as a woman. The masculine would no longer enter into the body or the flesh of the symbol but fashion it or pass it from hand to hand from the outside.

The bond between or the function shared by the pieces would be achieved secretly thanks to the female; the exchange of symbols would be assured by the masculine. By serving in this way as mediation from within the symbol, the feminine would have no access to sharing, exchanging, or coining symbols. In particular, the mother-daughter relationship, the attraction between mother and daughter, would be hidden in the symbol. Daughters, wives, and indeed mothers would not have, or would no longer have, signs available for their own relationships, or the means of designating a reality transcendent to themselves—their Other, their God or divine being. No articulated language would help women escape from the sameness of man or from an uninhabitable sameness of their own, lacking a passage from the inside to the outside of themselves, among themselves. Because they are used in mediation, as mediators, women can have within themselves and among themselves a *same*, an *Other* only if they move out of the existing systems of exchange. Their only recourse is flight, explosion, implosion, into an immediate relationship to nature or to God.

The cultural functions that women might have performed have been judged asocial and hence have been barred to them. They were accused of being *witches*, or *mystics*, because of the potency of the relations they maintained with the cosmos and the divine, even though they lacked any extrinsic or intrinsic

---

[11] See my "Women on the Market," in *This Sex Which Is Not One* (Ithaca: Cornell University Press, 1985), pp. 170–91.

way to express them, or express themselves. Useful in the elaboration of the Other of the masculine world, women could have only a forbidden Other of their own. Which was often called demonic possession whereas in fact it involves an ability to perceive the divine (*daimon*) to which man in his shell, his various shells, remains a stranger. In so far as he is alien to a sensible transcendental—the dimension of the divine par excellence—and of its grace, man would remain a little outside the religious world, unless he is initiated into it by women. And this happens in certain traditions. Even in our own, if one knows how to read certain texts: from the New Testament, from the Song of Songs, from the mystics, and so on. Given that our "tradition" is in fact a sedimentation laid down in its time by earlier traditions.

The sameness of women, among women, would always occur from and within *openness*, expansion. Generation. Threshold. Their Other without capital letters. Which is not to say that it has no reality or dimension that goes beyond the capital letters. Perhaps going beyond certain graphics or discourses already written down and consecrated? A cosmic, creative fermentation that is always and forever free. Though this is not it say it has no signs, no rhythms, no symbols, no god(s).

An Ethics of
Sexual Difference

Coming to Rotterdam to teach philosophy represents some-thing rather special. An adventure of thought, an adventure of discovery, or rediscovery, in a country that has offered a haven to several philosophers. Offered them tolerance and encourage-ment in their work. Outside of any dogmatic passion. In most cases.

Astonishingly, yet correlatively, these philosophers were of-ten interested in passion. And it is almost a tradition that Hol-land should be the territory where the issue of the passions is raised.

I shall not fail that history. Or rather, that history, knowingly or not, consciously or not, has chosen me, this year, to speak, in Rotterdam, in a course titled "The Ethics of the Passions." It is as if a certain necessity has led me to this part of the Netherlands to speak on this topic.

To each period corresponds a certain way of thinking. And even though the issues relating to passion and its ethics which need careful consideration today are still clearly linked to Des-cartes's *wonder* and Spinoza's *joy*, the perspective is no longer the

(This is the text of the public lecture, delivered November 18, 1982, which Irigaray refers to in the prefatory material of this book. In this highly allusive *tour d'horizon*, Irigaray gives no references.—Tr.)

same. This change in perspective is, precisely, a matter of ethics. We are no longer in an era where the subject reconstitutes the world in solitude on the basis of one fixed point: Descartes's certainty that he is a man. This is no longer the era of Spinoza, who wrote: "It is easy to see that if men and women together assumed political authority, peace would suffer great harm from the permanent probability of conflict."

Perhaps we need to reconsider Hegel's analysis of the ethical world and the interpretation of sexual difference he founds on the brother-sister couple he borrows from ancient tragedy: a couple in which sexual difference seems to find harmony through the neutering of the passion "of the blood," through suspension of the carnal act. A couple whose fecundity, while loving, leads to real death. A couple forming the substrate for both the conceptualization and realization of the family and of the state which still hold sway today.

But, in this couple, whereas the brother is still able to see himself in his sister as if she were a living mirror, she finds in him no image of herself that would allow her to leave the family and have a right to the "for-itself" of the spirit "of daylight." It is understood that she accedes to generality through her husband and her child but only at the price of her singularity. She would have to give up her sensibility, the singularity of her desire, in order to enter into the immediately universal of her family duty. Woman would be wife and mother without desire. Pure obligation dissociates her from her affect.

This duty, abstract and empty of all feeling, is supposedly at the root of woman's identity, once the sister is dead and the chorus of women has been buried under the town so that the order of the city-state may be founded.

An ethical imperative would seem to require a practical and theoretical revision of the role historically allotted to woman. Whereas this role was still interpreted by Freud as anatomic destiny, we need to understand that it has been determined by the necessities of a traditional sociocultural organization—one admittedly in the process of evolving today.

Philosophy, thought, and discourse do not evolve swiftly enough in response to "popular" movements. One of the places in our time where we can locate a people is the "world of women." Nonetheless, if there is to be neither repression of this "people" nor ethical error on its part, an access to sexual difference becomes essential, and society must abandon the murderous hierarchy as well as the division of labor which bars woman from accomplishing the task reserved for her by Hegel: the task of going from the deepest depths to the highest heavens. In other words, of being faithful to a process of the divine which passes through her, whose course she must needs sustain, without regressing or yielding up her singular desire or falling prisoner to some fetish or idol of the question of "God." Could it be that one of the qualities of this divine process is to leave woman open, her threshold free, with no closure, no dogmatism? Could this be one of its ethical deeds, in sexual exchange as well?

This opportunity to question the ethical status of sexual difference is the result of an invitation to give the lecture series established in honor of Jan Tinbergen—a man who set himself the task, among others, of trying to solve certain socioeconomic problems of the third world. If I take this occasion to broach the problem of the sociocultural situation of women (sometimes referred to as the fourth world), at the request of women, and thanks to them, it will, I hope, be seen as a gesture of respect toward a vocation of generosity that is the motivation for this lectureship dedicated to theoretical research and social practice.

So let me return to the character of Antigone, though I shall not identify with it. Antigone, the antiwoman, is still a production of a culture that has been written by men alone. But this figure, who, according to Hegel, stands for ethics, has to be brought out of the night, out of the shadow, out of the rock, out of the total paralysis experienced by a social order that condemns itself even as it condemns her. Creon, who has forbidden burial for Polynices, who has suggested that Antigone keep quiet from now on about her relations with the gods, Creon who has ordered Antigone to be closed up in a hole in the rock, leaving just a little food so that he cannot be guilty of her death—this Creon has condemned society to a split in the order of reason that leaves nature without gods, without grace. Leaves the family with no future other than work for the state, procreation without joy, love without ethics.

Creon, the king, will, in the end, endure a fate as cruel as Antigone's. But he will be master of that destiny.

Antigone is silenced in her action. Locked up—paralyzed, on the edge of the city. Because she is neither master nor slave. And this upsets the order of the dialectic.

She is not a master, that much is clear.

She is not a slave. Especially because she does nothing by halves. Except for her suicide, perhaps? Suicide, the only act left to her. Given that society passes—as Hegel would say—onto the side of darkness when it is a question of the right of the female to act.

But who would dare condemn Antigone?

Not those who denied her air, love, the gods, and even the preparation of food.

Antigone has nothing to lose. She makes no attempt on another's life. Hence the fear she arouses in Creon, who, for his part, has much at risk. I am no longer a man, he says; she is the man if I let her live. These words reveal the nature or the very essence of his crime. For him, the king, the only values are masculine, virile ones. Creon takes a risk when he wounds the other, the female, in the worship of her gods, in her right to love, to conscience, to speech. This wound will come back to haunt him as that abyss, that chasm, that night inscribed in the very heart of the dialectic, of reason, of society. Chasm or night that demands attention, like a "calvary" or a "chalice," writes Hegel.

If society today is afraid of certain men or certain women, we might ask ourselves what "crime" against them that fear might connote. And wonder if it is impossible to "imprison" or silence more than half of the world's population, for example.

This is all the more true when sensitivity becomes specularization, speculation, discourses that enter a loop of mutual interaction or lose their substance by depriving themselves of what once fed them, or fed them anew. Man is forced to search far and wide, within his memory, for the source of meaning. But by moving back into the past one risks losing the future. Discourse is a tight fabric that turns back upon the subject and wraps around and imprisons him in return. It is as if Agamemnon no longer needed Clytemnestra to catch him in her toils: discourse is net enough for him.

In the end, every "war" machine turns against the one who made it. At least according to Hegel? At least according to a certain logic of conscience? Unless we can pass into another?

Unless, at every opportunity, we ourselves take the negative upon ourselves. Which would amount to allowing the other his/her liberty, and sex. Which would assume that we accept losing ourselves by giving ourselves. Which would leave the decision about time to us. By giving us control over the debts we lay *on the future*.

Do we still have the time to face those debts?

Ethically, we have to give ourselves the time. Without forgetting to plan. Giving ourselves time is to plan on abjuring our deadly polemics so that we have time for living, and living together.

This ethical question can be approached from different perspectives, if I give myself, give us, time to think it through.

Given that *science* is one of the last figures, if not the last figure, used to represent absolute knowledge, it is—ethically— essential that we ask science to reconsider the nonneutrality of the supposedly universal subject that constitutes its scientific theory and practice.

In actual fact, the self-proclaimed universal is the equivalent of an idiolect of men, a masculine imaginary, a sexed world. With no neuter. This will come as a surprise only to an out-and-out defender of idealism. It has always been men who spoke and, above all, wrote: in science, philosophy, religion, politics.

But, nothing is said about scientific intuition (except by a few rare scientists, notably physicists). Intuition would apparently arise ex nihilo, aseptic as by right. And yet a few modalities or qualities of that intuition can be sorted out. It is always a matter of:

— Positing *a* world in front of the self, constituting a world *in front of the self.*

— Imposing *a model* on the universe so as to take possession of it, an abstract, invisible, intangible model that is *thrown over* the universe like an encasing garment. Which amounts to clothing the universe in one's own identity. One's own blindness, perhaps?

— Claiming that, as a subject, one is rigorously alien to the model, i.e., to prove that the model is purely and simply *objective.*

— Demonstrating that the model is "insensible" when in fact it has virtually been prescribed at least by the privilege accorded to the *visual* (i.e., by the absence, the distancing, of a subject that is yet surreptitiously there).

[*121*]

— A move out of the world of the senses made possible by the *mediation of the instrument*, the intervention of a technique that separates the subject from the object under investigation. A process of moving away and delegating power to something that intervenes between the universe observed and the observing subject.

— Constructing an *ideal* or *idea-generated* model, independent of the physical and mental makeup of its producer. With games of induction, as well as deduction, passing through an ideal elaboration.

— Proving the *universality* of the model, at least within a given time. And its absolute power (independent of its producer), its constitution of a unique and total world.

— Buttressing that *universality* by protocols of experiments which at least two (identical?) subjects must agree on.

— Proving that the discovery is *efficient, productive, profitable, exploitable* (or is it rather *exploitative* of a natural world increasingly drained of life?). Which is assumed to mean *progress*.

These characteristics reveal an "isomorphism with man's sexual imaginary." Which has to to be kept strictly under wraps. "Our subjective experiences or our personal opinions can never be used to justify any statement," claims the epistemologist of science.

But it is apparent in many ways that the subject in science is not neuter or neutral. Particularly in the way certain things are not discovered at a given period as well as in the research goals that science sets, or fails to set, for itself. Thus, in a more or less random list that refuses to respect the hierarchy of the sciences:

— *The physical sciences* constitute research targets in regard to a nature which they measure in an ever more formal, abstract, and modeled fashion. Their techniques, based on more and more sophisticated axiom-building, concern a matter which certainly still exists but cannot be perceived by the subject operating the experiment. At least in most sectors of these sciences. And "nature," the stake of the physical sciences, risks being exploited and torn apart at the hands of the physicist, even without his knowing. Given that the Newtonian dividing line has led scientific inquiry into a "universe" in which perception by the senses has almost no validity and which may even entail annulling precisely the thing that is at stake in the object of physics: the matter (whatever the predicates of matter may be) of the universe and of the bodies constituting it.

Within this very theory, in fact, there are deep divisions: theory of quanta/theory of fields, solid mechanics/fluid dynamics, for example. But the fact that the matter under study is inaccessible to the senses often involves the paradoxal privilege accorded to "solidity" in the discoveries, and science has been slow, or has even given up, trying to analyze the in-finite of force fields. Could this be interpreted as a refusal to take into account the dynamics of the subject researching himself?

— *The mathematical sciences*, in set theory, take an interest in closed and open spaces, in the infinitely large and infinitely small. They are less concerned with the question of the half-open, of fluid sets, of anything that analyzes the problem of edges, of the passage between things, of the fluctuations taking place from one threshold to the other of defined sets. (Even if topology raises such issues, does it not place far more emphasis on that which closes up than on that which remains without possible circularity?)

— *The biological sciences* have been very slow to take on certain problems. The constitution of the placental tissue, the permeability of membranes, for example. Are these not questions directly correlated to the female and the maternal sexual imaginary?

— *The logical sciences* are more concerned with bivalent theories than with trivalent or polyvalent ones. Is that because the latter still appear marginal? Because they upset the discursive economy?

— *The linguistic sciences* have concerned themselves with models for utterances, with synchronic structures of speech, with language models "known intuitively to any normally constituted subject." They have not faced, and at times even refuse to face, the question of the sexuation of discourse. They accept, perforce, that certain items of vocabulary may be added to the established lexicon, that new stylistic figures may potentially become acceptable, but they refuse to consider that syntax and the syntactic-semantic operation might be sexually determined, might not be neuter, universal, unchanging.

— *Economics* and perhaps even the social sciences have preferred to emphasize the phenomenon of scarcity and the question of survival rather than that of abundance and life.

— *Psychoanalytic science* is based on the two first principles of thermodynamics that underlie Freud's model of the libido. However, these two principles seem more isomorphic to male sexuality than to female. Given that female sexuality is less subject to alternations of tension-discharge, to conservation of required energy, to maintaining states of equilibrium, to functioning as a closed circuit that opens up through saturation, to the reversibility of time, etc.

If a scientific model is needed, female sexuality would perhaps fit better with what Prigogine calls "dissipatory" structures, which function through exchanges with the exterior world, which proceed in steps from one energy level to another, and which are not organized to search for equilibrium but rather to cross thresholds, a procedure that corresponds to going beyond disorder or entropy without discharge.

As we face these claims, these questions, this issue arises: *either* to do science *or* to become "militant." Or is it rather: to continue to do science *and* to divide oneself into several functions, several persons or characters? Should the "truth" of science and that of life remain separate, at least for the majority of researchers? What science or what life is at issue here, then? Particularly since life in our era is largely dominated by science and its techniques.

What is the origin of this split imposed and suffered by scientists? Is it a model of the subject that has not been analyzed? A "subjective" revolution that has not taken place? Given that the disintegration of the subject is programmed by the *episteme* and the power structures it has set up. Must we assume that the Copernican revolution has occurred but that the epistemological subject has yet to act on it and move beyond it? The discourse of the subject has been altered but finds itself even more disturbed by this revolution than the language of the world which preceded it. Given that the scientist, now, wants to be *in front of* the world: naming the world, making its laws, its axioms. Manipulating nature, exploiting it, but forgetting that he too is *in* nature. That he is still *physical*, and not only when faced with phenomena whose *physical* nature he tends to ignore. As he progresses according to an objective method designed to shelter him from any instability, any "mood," any feelings and affective fluctuations, from any intuition that has not been programmed in the name of science, from any influence of his desire, particularly his *sexual* desires, over his discoveries. Perhaps by installing himself within a system, within something that can be assimilated to what is already dead? Fearing, sterilizing the losses of equilibrium even though these are necessary to achieve a new horizon of discovery.

One of the ways most likely to occasion an interrogation of the scientific horizon is to question discourse about the subject of science, and the psychic and sexuate involvement of that subject in scientific discoveries and their formulation.

An Ethics of Sexual Difference

Such questions clamor to be answered, or at least raised, from somewhere outside, from a place in which the subject has not or has scarcely begun to be spoken. An outside placed on the other slope of sexual difference, the one which, while useful for reproducing the infrastructure of social order, has been condemned to imprisonment and silence within and by society. It remains true that the feminine, in and through her language, can, today, raise questions of untold richness. Still she must be allowed to speak; she must be heeded.

This may lead to the avoidance of two ethical mistakes, if I may return again to Hegel:

— Subordinating women to destiny without allowing them any access to mind, or consciousness of self and for self. Offering them only death and violence as their part.

— Closing man away in a consciousness of self and for self that leaves no space for the gods and whose discourse, even today and for that same reason, goes in search of its meaning.

In other words, in this division between the two sides of sexual difference, one part of the world would be searching for a way to find and speak its meaning, its side of signification, while the other would be questioning whether meaning is still to be found in language, values, and life.

This desperately important question of our time is linked to an injustice, an ethical mistake, a debt still owing to "natural law" and to its gods.

If this question is apparent in the dereliction of the feminine, it is also raised on the male side, in quest for its meaning. Humanity and humanism have proved that their ethos is difficult to apply outside certain limits of tolerance. Given that the world is not undifferentiated, not neuter, particularly insofar as the sexes are concerned.

The meaning that can be found on the male side is perhaps that of a debt contracted toward the one who gave and still gives man life, in language as well.

Language, however formal it may be, feeds on blood, on flesh, on material elements. Who and what has nourished language? How is this debt to be repaid? Must we produce more and more formal mechanisms and techniques which redound on man, like the inverted outcome of that mother who gave him a living body? And whom he fears in direct ratio to the unpaid debt that lies between them.

To remember that we must go on living and creating worlds is our task. But it can be accomplished only through the combined efforts of the two halves of the world: the masculine and the feminine.

And I shall end with an example of something that can constitute or entail an unpaid debt to the maternal, the natural, the matrical, the nourishing.

As we move farther away from our condition as living beings, we tend to forget the most indispensable element in life: *air*. The air we breathe, in which we live, speak, appear; the air in which everything "enters into presence" and can come into being.

This air that we never think of has been borrowed from a birth, a growth, a *phusis* and a *phuein* that the philosopher forgets.

To forget being is to forget the air, this first fluid given us gratis and free of interest in the mother's blood, given us again when we are born, like a natural profusion that raises a cry of pain: the pain of a being who comes into the world and is abandoned, forced henceforth to live without the immediate assistance of another body. Unmitigated mourning for the intrauterine nest, elemental homesickness that man will seek to assuage through his work as builder of worlds, and notably of the dwelling which seems to form the essence of his maleness: language.

In all his creations, all his works, man always seems to neglect thinking of himself as flesh, as one who has received his body as that primary home (that *Gestell*, as Heidegger would say, when, in "Logos," the seminar on Heraclitus, he recognizes that what metaphysics has not begun to address is the issue of the body) which determines the possibility of his coming into the world and the potential opening of a horizon of thought, of poetry, of celebration, that also includes the god or gods.

The fundamental dereliction in our time may be interpreted as our failure to remember or prize the element that is indispensable to life in all its manifestations: from the lowliest plant and animal forms to the highest. Science and technology are reminding men of their careless neglect by forcing them to consider the most frightening question possible, the question of a radical polemic: the destruction of the universe and of the human race through the splitting of the atom and its exploitation to achieve goals that are beyond our capacities as mortals.

"Only a god can save us now," said Heidegger, who was also remembering the words of Hölderlin, the poet with whom his thought was indissolubly linked. Hölderlin says that the god comes to us on a certain *wind* that blows from the icy cold of the North to the place where every sun rises: the East. The god arrives on the arms of a wind that sweeps aside everything that blocks the light, everything that separates fire and air and covers all with imperceptible ice and shadow. The god would refer back to a time before our space-time was formed into a closed world by an economy of natural elements forced to bow to man's affect and will. Demiurge that could have closed up the universe into a circle, or an egg, according to Empedocles.

Man's technical prowess today allows him to blow up the world just as, at the dawn of our culture, he was able to establish a finite horizon to it.

Is a god what we need, then? A god who can upset the limits of the possible, melt the ancient glaciers, a god who can make a future for us. A god carried on the breath of the *cosmos*, the song of the poets, the respiration of lovers.

We still have to await the god, remain ready and open to prepare a way for his coming. And, with him, for ourselves, to prepare, not an implacable decline, but a new birth, a new era in history.

Beyond the circularity of discourse, of the nothing that is in and of being. When the copula no longer veils the abyssal burial of the other in a gift of language which is neuter only in that it forgets the difference from which it draws its strength and energy. With a neuter, abstract *there is* giving way to or making space for a "we are" or "we become," "we live here" together.

This creation would be our opportunity, from the humblest detail of everyday life to the "grandest," by means of the opening of a *sensible transcendental* that comes into being through us, of which *we would be* the mediators and bridges. Not only in mourning for the dead God of Nietzsche, not waiting passively for the god to come, but by conjuring him up among us, within us, as resurrection and transfiguration of blood, of flesh, through a language and an ethics that is ours.

❧ IV

Love of the Other

Traces or Symptoms of Sexual Difference in Language

We are living in an era when, at any rate in most cases, scholars still claim that discourse and truth are neutral, and that the attempt to show that they have a sex and bear sex markers is "poetry," "demagogy," "utopia," "madness," "foolishness," and so on. The claim is that truth and scientific laws are *neutral* and *universal*. The subject who enunciates the law is, they tell us, irrelevant, bodiless, morphologically undetermined. The question of what the source of the subject's enunciation of this *episteme* might be fades away unanswered. A question that is difficult to raise without tracking down the "subject" in a net that secures him without his realizing it: the net of a language which he believes he controls but which controls him, imprisons him in a bodiless body, in a fleshless other, in laws whose cause, source, and physical, living reason he has lost. The subject is determined by the various forms, living or dead, budding or hidebound, which he reproduces, often unawares. The subject is ignorant or uncomprehending of language's capacity to generate, to procreate symbols.

To prove that discourse has a sex amounts to a show of force, and its outcome is challenged even when the most rigorous and scientific standards of proof are followed. Here even the most respectable statistical investigations risk a rough reception, in spite of their traditional methodology. The stakes are so high that everything is subject to denial, incomprehension, blindness, rejection.

Therefore, in spite of the curiosity, the even passionate interest such research arouses, the results of a systematic inquiry into the sexuation of language are still treated with vague suspicion. Is this a reversal, a "return of the repressed," of the mastery over language exercised by one sex?

Nonetheless, a certain number of investigations into this matter are under way today.

My own work on the language of those suffering from dementia and schizophrenia has led me to question certain groups of neurotics (and which of us is not neurotic?) from the perspective of sexual difference, a difference that was already emerging in the results obtained from my initial analysis of the language of demented and schizophrenic patients—even though this difference was in no way the research target I had set myself.[1] Thus, it has only been at a second stage in my research that I have carried out analysis of spoken discourse based on the utterances of male subjects, on the one hand, and female subjects, on the other. The results offer a truth that is both commonplace and surprising and that could not have been predicted from the protocols.

The typical sentence produced by a male, once all substitutions have been allowed for, is:

I wonder if I am loved or: *I tell myself that perhaps I am loved.*
The typical sentence produced by a woman is:

Do you love me?

---

[1] See Luce Irigaray, *Le langage des déments* (The Hague: Mouton, 1973) and *Parler n'est jamais neutre* (Paris: Minuit, 1985).

In the first case, the utterance circles back to the speaker with the almost constant wariness of a *doubt*. The subject speaks to himself. Doubt is often the only weak point in the bubble in which he is situated and enclosed. No place for words for the other here. The message is reflexive, reflects back to the one who produces, or reproduces, it. The medium, the imagery of the message is so closely involved with the speaker that should another person, male or female, wish to try to listen, even without being invited, he or she would have great difficulty understanding what is being said.

The other is excluded from the communication in two ways: as speaker and as listener; the other can only shout an appeal or ask a question: *do you love me?* (correlative to *who am I?*). The interrogative form presents the message as ambiguous, incomplete. The *yes* or the *no* of the (you) underlies the meaning of the utterance, and the only subject of utterance here is the person addressed. The subject who is apparently producing the message occurs only as the possible *object* of the person addressed, an object that is no longer a point of convergence for the protagonists of the utterance, an object of exchange, because the only subject is (you).

These two types of utterances are incomplete from the point of view of both addressor and addressee, and they raise the issue of the differentiation of the poles of utterance. For the (I) and the (you) are distinct from one another in function of a singular reference to the world, and they "divide" up the world, but in a way that hinders communication. They represent two unequal parts of the world that are capable neither of exchange nor of alliance. A kind of original symbol that has been badly split and which deteriorates into various pathologies as a result of that badly managed separation or fission.

This leads to social crises, to individual illnesses, to schematic and fossilized identities for both sexes, as well as to a general sclerosis of discourse, a hardening of language and a repetitiveness that makes nonsense of established meaning. Inflation and devaluation afflict a semantic system installed in a position it refuses to question.

Anyone who denies that discourse is sexed is advised to carry out a statistical investigation of taped materials and analyze the results. If he still claims to discern no difference, then his own interpretation would have to be analyzed to see how it reproduces one of the patterns of the taped material, even, or perhaps especially, in the denials.[2]

Quite apart from these pathological utterances (assuming that there is such a thing as a normal utterance), I have also done some work on sentences produced by psychology students of the science faculty of the University of Lyon. A trigger word was given to a group of male students and a group of female students. The differences between the two groups are apparent not only in the meaning of the utterances but also in their structuring. Their sentence constructions, transformations, and modalities are not the same. For example, negative expressions are much more frequent with men, and interrogative expressions with women. This is just one example. It would take too long to give a complete report on this research at this stage. I simply wanted to point to the existence of this work as a basis of information not deriving from research into linguistic pathology.

These givens of speech, these dramatic scenes played out between "I" and "you," are often masked in the words we hear every day. In fact, masculine utterances have generally already been transformed into *the third person*. In this way the subject is masked by and within the world, the truth. But this universe is the subject's construction. The *he* is a transformation, a trans-

---

[2] A longer form of this analysis, entitled "Toward a Grammar of the Utterances of Hysterical and Obsessional Patients," can be found in Irigaray, *Parler n'est jamais neutre*, pp. 55–68. This paper was first published in the journal *Langages*, no. 5 (March 1967).

position of the *I*. Which uses the edifice of language to blur the enunciation. And denies also who it is who has produced this grammar, this meaning, and the rules governing them.

This *he* can also turn into a *there is*, one more mask for the *I*. Or a translation of the energies of a world, of a *you* that is more or less independent of the subject. On the surface no one is responsible for the discourse. A truth that would be neutral, aseptic, universal. With a director hidden in the wings. Or else situated in God, perhaps? Or so far back in the past that we no longer know the secret of his archives. Language would have become a kind of second nature for man or an autonomous nature, as if it had been constructed, spoken, and talked independently of the subject. As if it had fallen from the sky or grown out of the earth? And the assumption here would be that this language, if by chance this were possible, is a mimesis of the macrocosm. With certain elements forgotten? A certain sex forgotten? Or a relation between micro- and macrocosm? This structure of language loses its properties, its propriety, once there is the slightest degree of pathology in the subject. Then there is a reemergence of language's infrastructure and of the drama of utterance which is habitually concealed. Thus the redundance of the *I* on the "masculine" side and the circularity of the process of utterance constitute the world in a tautological circle.

This unveiling can also be triggered by a social crisis. And the women's movements are one manifestation of this. Often using gestures, slogans, cries and pleas and shouts of emotion, women are saying that they want to have complete access to discourse. To become "I"s who produce truth: cultural, political, religious truth. They translate their desire in a somewhat naively empirical way because they lack that sustained practice in discursive relations to the world and to the other which might have led them to protect themselves from a *he-she*, or motivated them to work out some kind of *there is*. Women remain at the threshold of utterance in a speech that is almost devoid of meaning: they chatter, gossip, laugh, shout. . . . Are women the guardians of the phonetics of language, of sounds? Between noise and singing. Each woman alone, or together. Whatever the deep significance of this enunciatory practice may be, women wish to achieve a praxis of meaning. They have taken over the word and thereby exposed the circularity of "male" discourse, unmasked its rituals and failures. But this movement still encounters considerable resistance, and it is still at an inceptive stage. One reason may be that woman finds herself with this choice: *either you are a woman or you speak-think.*

Economy of Signs

Often, in his own tongue, man describes, narrates, states, collects, organizes. He doubles the world or creates it. He may even happen to stage a dialogue. But he remains the creator or engenderer of the universe, and of discourse, even when he mimes or repeats a truth that he does not really accept.

Woman, for her part, chats, tattles, gossips, weaves inventions, fables, myths. She exchanges the means of exchange without having any object. Or does she make statements without having any fixed stake in what she has stated? Forever in the utterance? There is something *between* "subjects" without "objects" other than language itself. Some sharing or some communion of words that does not rely on the message of the communication? *The message is the communication.* She remains within the communication as if in depths whose forms are not always clear-cut, not univocal. She says. But what? Saying itself? And when she is obliged to be "clear," in the traditional mode of the clarity of truth, she tries to do "as well as," "like" that which has already been produced of the world. Does she repeat the repetition of the other? Not create her world? Her truth? Always in the mode of questioning? But how is the question to be raised, placed, when the other closes, encircles, surrounds the truth, the world, the whole?

Does man's discourse not open up in the direction of his *God*? The modalities of the utterances or sentences which imply or signify the act of a "dialogue"—are they not used in the relation to God? In commands, prayers, appeals, graces, cries, dirges, glorias, anger, and questions? Performatives, the means of gaining access to the presence of the other, to the relation to the other in and through language, as well across time, are habitually reserved for the relations between man and his God, and not for the exchange between men and women as others.

Rarely is the question "Who art thou?" asked of anyone (male or female) other than God. And the question is stated, often with no clear articulation, in such a way as to remain without possible response. (Thus: "*I am he who,*" or "*that which,*" follows but does not answer a question; it constitutes an affirmation that goes beyond or falls short of any dialogue.) The question signifies entry into a world. If woman replies or tries to reply to the interpellation regarding what she is, she throws the order of discourse into confusion. She is not replying to the question "*Who art thou?*" from within, in the context of the discourse of man, of humanity. She replies elsewhere. With or on the basis of another language, another world, a different relation to being. Often situated on the side of the abyss, perhaps, that other slope of the transcendence of the God? Where being in the feminine is to become, to grow unchecked. Without ecstasy or standing outside the self, if she is faithful to herself. Rather, *standing within* a world of the senses which arises and reroots itself, continuously. Language forever close to a *vegetal* blossoming. Designed and shaped to remain linked to natural rhythms and configurations? A reflexion, whether symmetrical or not, inscribed in the vegetal before any subjective mirror has been imposed, interposed.

[*139*]

The energy of utterance would thus be:

— secured for the constitution and maintenance of the world (in a sort of substitutive subjectivity: with the word of language, the world as language, being the home-subject);

— transformed in order to be addressed to the God according to various modes;

— consumed, assimilated, on the basis of some reserves that the "I" would draw upon and re-echo, reserves from below or from on high between which he would attempt to metabolize-economize a split.

The end of a culture would correspond also to the death of God. Which God? He who forms the transcendental keystone of a discourse used by a single gender, of a monosexed truth. And this would allow the return of the divine, of the god who preaches neither truth nor morality but would seek to live with us and allow us to live here. The cries and words of the last philosophers, of Nietzsche and Heidegger, about the "death of God" are a summons for the divine to return as festival, grace, love, thought. Contrary to the usual interpretation made of them, these philosophers are not talking about the disappearance of the gods but about the approach or the annunciation of another parousia of the divine. Which involves the remolding of the world, of discourse: another morning, a new era in history, in the universe. The end of times, and the access to one time, to one space-time, that are different.

Could this be the time when a meeting between the sexes becomes possible? For the fact that man and woman have not spoken to each other—not since the first garden?—is expressed also through the extinction of voice in discourse, the forgetting of voice in language. The forever unstable modulation of truth, which marks the index of sexedness in speech. A truth would have no place to exist or insist if it had no voice. In our culture, the voice has been abandoned to song, as if speech could remain without voice. From the voice of Yahweh to that or those of Antigone, of Persephone, of the Erinyes, the voices have been silenced. The text of the law, of all laws, holds sway in silence. With no trace inscribed in the flesh. Outside of current dialogue. Is law merely the memory of a passage? Awaiting an incarnation? or reincarnation?

Relation to the World and to Its Space-time

To inhabit is the fundamental trait of man's being. Even if this trait remains unconscious, unfulfilled, especially in its ethical dimension, man is forever searching for, building, creating homes for himself everywhere: caves, huts, women, cities, language, concepts, theory, and so on.

To perceive—is this the usual dimension of the feminine? Of women, who, it seems, remain within perception without need of name or concept. Without closure. To remain within perception means staying out in the open, always attuned to the outside, to the world. Senses always alert. Does woman sometimes cleave to the universe? Without necessarily being shared between two brightnesses, two nights. To perceive, to remain within the perception of the world without closing it off or closing off the self, amounts to forming or watching over the *threshold* of the world. Changing in response to the era, to place, to time. And the hardest thing would be to constitute a memory in the space where man at times closes himself off inside a *pathos* of memory, inside a nostalgia that forgets the threshold, the flesh.

There is a *pathos* of remembering and forgetting. Moving backward in search of something that has been erased, or inscribing it so that it shall not be erased. Fretting over repetitions, reproductions, over what has been erased and comes back. A sort of double nature or revolt of nature rising up through language.

Repetition can be a move backward for a choice, a new junction, a better road. It can be the pathetic, urgent call of something cut off from its roots and dying, which is repeated twice and then endlessly, for lack of the sap needed for growth.

The pathology of memory may correspond to a historical pathology. Psychoanalysis, in particular, shows us that, just as it is impossible to suppress "the gods of the underworld," so we cannot, short of death or a turning back, annihilate our living roots.

And even as man, consciously or unconsciously, feeds on and exploits the maternal-feminine in order to live, survive, inhabit, work, he forgets the other and his own becoming. He arrests his growth and repeats, endlessly, searching for the moment when the separation of memory and forgetting was lost to him. But, the more he repeats, the more he surrounds himself with envelopes, containers, "houses" which prevent him from finding either the other or himself. His nostalgia for a first and last dwelling prevents him from meeting and living with the other. Nostalgia blocks the threshold of the ethical world. It does so with the *currency-tool which is used* for inhabiting and sheltering the other. But money cannot support life. However necessary, money is no substitute for life. Giving money to the other is no payment for the still virgin, available creature [*étant*] that the other uses to provide you with support, nourishment, space, and matter for creation, that creature that the other—male or female—would need and desire in return: to build an identity, a language, a body of work.

Sexuality and Technique

Perversion, which is often touted as a means of escape from repressive morality, remains the slave to a morality of sexual difference that is traditionally organized in a hierarchy and has been made better or worse by our technical world. The body today is cut into parts like a mechanical body. Energy is equated with work energy. This is no doubt part and parcel of our era or its willing accomplice but, for all its apparent progressiveness, it forgets or shuns the *flesh*.

The race to do work and the race to be sexually active are partners. Exhaustion at work and the relaxation-discharge of orgasm are partners. The same *body* is involved, the same relation to signs (*soma-sema*), though this does not mean that flesh is at issue here. The "world" controls the economic game, not the subject's intention and its encounter with the other. The world is in charge. The creator is at the beck and call of his creature or his creation. . . . No longer by his will, his want. Man has built himself a world that is largely uninhabitable. A world in his image? An uninhabitable functional body? Like the technical world and all its sciences. Or like the scientific world and all its techniques.

Looked at this way, it is not surprising that genital sexuality is despised by some men and women. Or scrutinized. But "partial" sexuality is also the slave to technique. For good and ill.

Partial sexuality touches, hears, sees, breathes, and tastes of "technique," of something prefabricated, reliant on technical means, in most cases. And the body is torn between the different speeds of perception that situate it. No doubt the body has always functioned according to differences in the speed of perception. But before there was always something global or earthly or elemental to hold it together.

Today, man would like to equal the machine. Consciously or unconsciously, he thinks of himself as a machine: a sexuality of drives, an energy governed by tensions and discharges, in good or bad working order, and so on. Something capable of uniting the different drives has been forgotten. Could it be something about love, and the thought of love? About an organic rhythm made possible by love that takes and gives time. A zone of calm and respite from the race toward productivity. In sexual matters as well. Something that resists dispersion, diaspora, the explosion of the flesh or of the incarnation. Nietzsche thought of the subject as an atom. This atom will be split if it fails to find some life-enhancing rhythm. Some economy for growing like a plant, as opposed to a simple plan of survival. And if man, in the era of science and technology, thinks of himself as a machine, or even an atomic machine—as we see in the discourse of biology, medicine, psychology, in language theories, and so on—perhaps he should ask himself at least two or three questions about his survival, or survival in general.

Surviving?

A word we often hear today, a bridge-word for our generation, a generation unable to think, create, or live for itself, is the word *survival*.

But does survival have a meaning? And isn't the meaning we give to it anti-Nietzschean, whereas its mode of usage comes to us from Nietzsche and his "disciples." For Nietzsche, to survive equals to live more, not to eke out a living. It means to master a style of life so that one may rediscover or else create new values. To go beyond man or exploit him like a bridge to reach the superman.

Surviving, in many conversations, in many places today means hibernating. Waiting. For what? Isn't it true that this kind of survival, this interpretation of surviving, still exhausts more or less quickly the reserves of that thing or being that is trying to live? Hasn't survival become a sort of petit bourgeois deal with life? In a West that seems to have lost its regulating questions: about the transcendental, about God, about the aporias we experience in regard to the problem of the infinite.

Who or what can move us out of mere survival except a return to the bodily-fleshly values that have never yet come to full flower? In order to unfold them "voluntarily." Since the great rhythms of incarnation, respiration, circulation of the blood, have never been taken on by man. Who never grows up. Who goes back to childhood in order to come to maturity. Freely cutting a sort of umbilical cord to the woman-mother, mother nature who was still breathing for him, still fed and warmed him, gave him a home, a nest. Continuance of life in the womb which seems to have its counterpoint in the hyper-technological world about which man is as *infans*, speechless, as he is about his mother?

If man became aware of this perpetual dependence and freely chose to take charge of his life, this would set up a space, a space-time for sexual difference. He would no longer be enveloped or assisted by the maternal, on the one hand, and would no longer treat the female as a kind of doll or robot, on the other? With no flesh in either case? If there is to be flesh, an autonomous breath must infuse the body. Through autonomous forms of life and love. Survival yokes the end of the world, the old age of man, with the mind-set of a babe in arms, unable to satisfy his own baby needs and desires. A kind of infantile parasite on the mother's care but a parasite who nonetheless rules the world?

If man—who claims to be humanity—is to escape from survival, he would thus need to escape from this mixture of old man and *infans* which is still his condition. Given, let me insist, that the increasing availability of medical care offers nothing but palliatives to the same mentality. Given the parallel or complementary risk and blackmail of war. A terrible game for adults that is still a children's game (is it children who play with guns, who play soldiers like adults, or is it adults who play like children?).

If man achieves autonomy from a maternal that supports him, from the kind of all-powerful Other that is finally extrapolated into God, then perhaps he will discover that there is something inhering in the female that is not maternal? Another body? Another machine? (At worst?) A machine that uses a different source of energy? Which would oblige man—humanity—to glimpse something other. Something not of his world. Not built to his specifications.

This would allow, or oblige, him to desist from assigning the female:

1. to *reproduction,* as a maternal machine designed to have babies, populate the home, but also keep it clean, supplied with food, etc.;

2. to the *guardianship of the dead,* as a kind of mute tomb for the sign-body, keeper of the hearth, "vestal" of the desire and the mind of man (especially as fetish?);

3. to becoming a kind of *mechanical doll* for lovemaking, with no affect save seductiveness. Which does not mean an affect "of her own," but one that is *for the other* and in exile from her *for self.* The seductiveness that woman or women exert over people is rarely a *for herself or themselves.* It serves rather to uproot the female from her condition of *in self*—as Hegel would say—by transforming her into a *for the other,* by carrying her away from her vegetal life, which is not nothing, so that she can be assigned to a public function (even if this is performed in private) which is nothing, except a way of keeping the machine turning;

4. to becoming *the incarnation of man's, or mankind's, fantasies*; so that she is the basis for inscription, the more or less living sculpture, the darkly encircling countryside, the goddess, the refuse heap, and so on.

Perhaps man might then discover that something of another world persists in the female. Something that lives. That is neither plant nor animal,[3] neither mother nor child simply. Something or someone other. So very different that he can have no

---

[3] See G. W. F. Hegel, *The Phenomenology of Mind,* trans. J. B. Baillie (New York: Harper Torchbooks, 1967), and Emmanuel Levinas, "Phenomenology of Eros," in *Totality and Infinity: An Essay on Exteriority,* trans. Alphonso Lingis (Pittsburgh: Duquesne University Press, 1969).

idea of it? Or else that—by bending that something to his idea—
he loses its power? Something so different that he has no
thought of it? Even in his sexual period? Which he still interprets
in terms of
— erection,
— ec-stasy, going out of himself (in the Other?),
— ejaculation, out of himself into the other.

Man, mankind, might take out a new lease on life if he were
to exploit something (notably something vegetal) that is neither
this nor that. Nothing that man has ever thought of or conceived: in self for self for him. Immanence, in-stance [*l'instance*]
in the feminine?

Parousia

Does parousia correspond to the expectation of a future not
only as a *utopia* or a *destiny* but also as a *here and now*, the willed
construction of a bridge in the present between the past and the
future?
A theology and indeed an ontology that were affirmative—
would these, quite apart from their working of the negative,
imply the coming or the parousia of God or of the other? Are
these two parousias not in fact inseparable? Would crossing
through the neuter—the space-time of remission of the polemic?—set up the return or reappearance of God or of the
other?
"I shall return at the end of time," says Christ, an era when
the spirit will come to the bride to seal the alliance of heaven
and earth. A new Pentecost, when fire—mingled perhaps with
wind?—will be given back to the female so that a world still to
come can be accomplished.
Why should this theology or theologality of hope remain a
utopia? Not an inscription in the flesh. *An atopia.* And why do

we pay least heed to those texts which speak of the return or the coming of God, of the other, as phenomena of the incarnation which are still unknown to us? Why do we consider these the least pure of the texts, the least trustworthy? Why do we assume that God must always remain an inaccessible transcendence rather than a realization—here and now—in and through the body? Like a transfiguration that would not be reduced to a moment, or like a resurrection that would not involve the disappearance of this world. With the spirit impregnating the body in and through a lasting alliance. Father, son, and spirit in one "person"? Three generations in one? Yielding to the bride through the mediation of a fire that is itself transmuted? Appearing anew, beyond idol, image, fetish, those representations that are still extrapolated from the body. With memory, expectation, still potentially blocking incarnation.

Waiting for parousia would require keeping all one's senses alert. Not destroyed, not covered, not "dirtied," our senses would be open. If God and the other are to be unveiled, then I too must unveil myself (I should not expect God to do this for me. Not this time. Even though I am doing this with, thanks to, and for Him). Let this be something I am able to do, without ever having done with it.

Keeping the senses alert means being attentive in flesh and in spirit.

The third era of the West might, at last, be the era of the *couple*: of the spirit and the bride? After the coming of the Father that is inscribed in the Old Testament, after the coming of the Son in the New Testament, we would see the beginning of the era of the spirit and the bride. With father and son summoned for the coming of this third stage in the parousia. The Father comes and disappears; the son comes and disappears; the incarnation of the spirit has never taken place except, prophetically, at Pentecost. The spirit appears as the third term. The term of alliance, of mediation? By fire?

— The Father, alone, invites, and disappears with Moses and the written law.

— The son (and the mother) invites; but the son remains bound to the Father, to whom he "goes back," to whom he arises.

— The spirit and the bride invite beyond genealogical destiny to the era of the wedding and the festival of the world. To the time of a theology of the breath in its horizontal and vertical becoming, with no murders.

As long as the son is not in mourning for the Father, neither body nor flesh can be transfigured in the couple; as long as the daughter is in mourning for the spirit, then neither body nor flesh can be transfigured in the couple.

The spirit is not to be imprisoned only in the Father-son duality. The spirit eludes this "couple." This event is announced in the Gospel itself: the female, the women partake not in the Last Supper but in the Pentecost, and it is they who discover and announce the resurrection. This seems to say that the body of man can return to life when woman no longer forgets that she has a share in the spirit. In this way her transfiguration would take place. The moment of her glorification, finally without masochism. Without the infliction of wounds. Without the need for her body to be opened over and again to pleasure, to jouissance, or to conception. The body would be enveloped in her flesh. Inside-outside.

Even for conception, the cradle would in some sense be ready. The nest for the child would be possible if the female had its own nest. If woman had her own territory: her birth, her genesis, her growth. With the female becoming in self and for self—as Hegel would say. An in self and a for self that are not closed off in the self-sufficiency of a consciousness or a mind. An in self and a for self that always also remain for the other and in a world and a universe that are partway open.

For woman to affirm that her desire proceeds or wills thus,

woman must be born into desire. She must be longed for, loved, valued as a daughter. An other morning, a new parousia that necessarily accompanies the coming of an ethical God.

He respects the difference between him and her, in cosmic and aesthetic generation and creation. Sharing the heaven and the earth in all their elements, potencies, acts.

The Invisible of the Flesh:
A Reading of Merleau-Ponty,
The Visible and the Invisible,
"The Intertwining—The Chiasm"

"If it is true that as soon as philosophy declares itself to be reflection or coincidence it prejudges what it will find, then once again it must recommence everything, reject the instruments reflection and intuition had provided themselves, and install itself in a locus where they have not yet been distinguished, in experiences that have not yet been 'worked over,' that offer us all at once, pell-mell, both 'subject' and 'object,' both existence and essence, and hence give philosophy resources to redefine them." (Maurice Merleau-Ponty, *The Visible and the Invisible,* p. 130).[1]

Up to this point, my reading and my interpretation of the history of philosophy agree with Merleau-Ponty: we must go back to a moment of prediscursive experience, recommence everything, all the categories by which we understand things, the world, subject-object divisions, recommence everything and pause at the "mystery, as familiar as it is unexplained, of a light which, illuminating the rest, remains at its source in obscurity."

---

[1] Page references following the quotations from Maurice Merleau-Ponty are to *The Visible and the Invisible,* trans. Alphonso Lingis (Evanston: Northwestern University Press, 1968).

"*If we could rediscover within the exercise of seeing and speaking some of the living references that assign themselves such a destiny in a language, perhaps they would teach us how to form our new instruments, and first of all to understand our research, our interrogation themselves.*" (P. 130).

This operation is absolutely necessary in order to bring the maternal-feminine into language: at the level of theme, motif, subject, articulation, syntax, and so on. Which requires passage through the night, a light that remains in obscurity.

"*The visible about us seems to rest in itself. It is as though our vision were formed in the heart of the visible, or as though there were between it and us an intimacy as close as between the sea and the strand.*" (Pp. 130–31).

If it were not the visible that was in question, it would be possible to believe that Merleau-Ponty is alluding here to intra-uterine life. Moreover, he uses "images" of the sea and the strand. Of immersion and emergence? And he speaks of the risk of the disappearance of the seer and the visible. Which corresponds doubly to a reality in intrauterine nesting: one who is still in this night does not see and remains without a visible (as far as we know); but the other seer cannot see him. The other does not see him, he is not visible for the other, who nevertheless sees the world, but without him. And if everything, the totality, is organized around him, then the other, one could almost say, sees nothing? A disorganized world? If the mother, or the woman, sees the world only from the perspective of the maternal function, she sees nothing. Except from this zero of the infant's nocturnal abode? The invisible of its prenatal life. This intimate secret of its-their birth and shared knowledge [*connaissance*]. What-had-not-yet-been-seen of and by its-their look. Seeing the universe in function of or beginning with that—

which will never appear as something seen within the field of the visible.

Perhaps it comes about that, out of his nostalgia, man wishes to see that which she does not see? Her own invisible? His return would also be the search for this night of hers. Wanting to appropriate two invisibles, two positions of the one in relation to the other where they touch without the possibility of seeing each other, and without for all that finding the one behind the other. A look forever organized, or disorganized, around an impossibility of seeing [*un impossible à voir*]. Insurmountable other of the visible, not reducible to its invisible other side. It is a question of another world, another landscape, a *topos* or a locus of the irreversible.

The next sentence can be understood in the open field through this interpretive gesture: if we based ourselves in this visible, or rather in its resting place [*repos*], its heart, and if it passed into us, vision would vanish at the moment of its formation through the disappearance of either the seer or the visible.

Thus: there is either no more seer, or subject, or no more world, or visible. Either the one or the other at opposite poles, antagonistic, adverse. Although he dismisses the subject and the object, Merleau-Ponty nevertheless retains this polarity: seer/visible, which presupposes, here in particular, that the visible, still invisible in its resting place, would have vision and could give it to or take it away from the seer. Later on, he says that the seer and the visible are reversible, that in a way they come back to the same thing, but after having set up this dissociation from the start: the risk of the disappearance of the one *or* the other.

What follows returns the privilege to the *seer's* look. But of a vision in between the diurnal and the nocturnal in its touch. A look that is too close to make use of a certain perspective, of discrimination, distancing, or mastery? A carnal look, which becomes that which gives perspective to "things": shelters them, gives birth to them, wraps them in the touch of a visibility that is one with them, keeps them from ever being naked, envelops them in a conjunctive tissue of visibility, an exterior-interior horizon in which, henceforth, they appear without being able to be distinguished, separated, or torn away from it.

"Whence does it happen that in so doing it leaves them in their place, that the vision we acquire of them seems to us to come from them, and that to be seen is for them but a degradation of their eminent being?" (P. 131).

Enveloping things with his look, the seer would give birth to them, and/yet the mystery of his own birth would subsist in them. For now they contain this mystery of the prenatal night where he was palpated without seeing. A passive forever lacking an active. More passive than any passivity taken in a passive-active couple. A passivity that tries to turn itself into activity by sculpting, moving the totality of the world into a reversion of the intrauterine abode. Between these two extremes, *there is* a breach: the place of the other. The seer tries to put back together the most passive and the most active, to overcome the invisible of/in the other insofar as it would constitute a night that his look needed to reduce in order to organize his field of vision. He tries to establish a *continuum*, a duration, between the most passive and the most active. But he cannot manage it. Especially without memory of that first event where he is enveloped-touched by a tangible invisible of which his eyes are also formed, but which he will never see: with no seer, neither visible nor visibility in that place.

Perhaps there exists, there is, a *foreseeing* where the maternal is concerned? Something that would make the child believe it is seen before it sees? That the invisible looks at it? And, if the mother foresees her child, imagines it, she foresees it also in this sense that the feeling of it within herself is sometimes transformed into vision: a clairvoyance of, and within, the flesh. Could it be that he uses this clairvoyance to surround things?

Constituting them as things, or reduplicating them as things, with that encompassing look with which he envelops them.

Whence does it happen that "to be seen is for them is a degradation of their eminent being"? Sight reduces the invisible of things and of the look, their tissue, their clothing of seeing flesh, that nostalgia for a first abode lodged in and on them, which will be twice lost: in the coming to being of the seer and, even more, in the look's becoming vision; in the envelopment of things in names and in a network of names, a language, from this point, this axis, where their "soul," their cloak of invisibility, their immiscion in a fleshly layering [*feuilleté*] is degraded, flattened? Which happens through their appearing only from a vantage point, a sort of photograph that puts them into the world while wrenching them from their surroundings, the thickness of their gestures, which are also visual. But once there, opened up to the contemplation of their unfolding?

"What is this talisman of color, this singular virtue of the visible that makes it, held at the end of the gaze, nonetheless much more than a correlative of my vision, such that it imposes my vision upon me as a continuation of its own sovereign existence?" (P. 131).

At this point, the talisman of color appears, with its "atmospheric" properties, which are irreducible to the form that seeing defines. Color? The symptom and aftereffect of our incarnation, our genetic fate, our identity prior to any proper form perceivable from outside, to any visible, which will nevertheless appear but without ever encompassing itself in its growth. Color? That by which I (male or female) am moreover affronted as if by a genealogical heritage that I cannot change: I can change neither the color of my eyes nor my vision of things or of the atmosphere that results from this color. Correlatively (?), from without, color signals to me that it holds sovereignty over the purchase or the influence of my gaze. That it allows me to see rather than that I make it conform to my decisions? That it pours itself out, extends itself, escapes, imposes itself upon me as the reminder of what is most archaic in me, the *fluid*. Through which I (male or female) received life and was enveloped in my prenatal sojourn, by which I have been surrounded, clothed, nourished, in another body. Thanks to which I could also see the light, be born, and even see: air, light. . . . Color resuscitates in me all of that prior life, the preconceptual, preobjective, presubjective, this *ground* of the visible where seeing and seen are not yet distinguished, where they reflect each other without any position having been established between them. Color bathes my gaze, which sees it, perceives it more or less well, changes it in its visibility, but can never delimit it, create it, bend it to its decisions. Color constitutes a given that escapes from the subjective realm and that still and always immerses the subject in an invisible sojourn of the visible, a sojourn that cannot be mastered: whether infernal or celestial, preceding or following a determinate incarnation into subject-object duality. This color, the correlative of my vision, of vision, far from being able to yield to my decisions, obliges me to see.

"*How does it happen that my look, enveloping them [things], does not hide them, and, finally, that, veiling them, it unveils them?*" (P. 131).

Following this detour by way of color, his sentence links up without a transition to what was being said about the vision of things. As if this passage on color had been only a parenthesis, whereas it will be developed at length. How should this construction be understood? What is its relation to the note at the bottom of the page? Not only is it a question of course notes here, and not really of a text, but the passage demonstrates an astonishing reversal: my gaze, which would receive itself from the visible, envelops things without hiding them and unveils them while veiling them. My gaze would be a connective tissue between the interior and the exterior. But formed inside (through "the incorporation of the seer into the visible"), even if

The Invisible of the Flesh

it is perfected outside. Formed within the living tissue of my body. On the inside prior to the constitution of its interior horizon. How do the inside of conception-organization and the inside of internal horizons mingle? Two leaves of my body and two leaves of the world seem to make it impossible for another flesh to be visible and seeing, between the one and the other. The subtlety of what is said of the visible and of its relation to the flesh does not rule out the solipsistic character of this touch(ing) between the world and the subject, of this touch(ing) of the visible and the seer in the subject itself.

Merleau-Ponty's whole analysis is marked by this labyrinthine solipsism. Without the other, and above all the other of sexual difference, isn't it impossible to find a way out of this description of the visible, doubled with that of the tactile of the touching hands? But unless we are to remain within the confines of this rigorous and luxuriant approach, we must ask the question of the other as touched and touching. And of an other whose body's ontological status would differ from my own.

"We must first understand that this red under my eyes is not, as is always said, a quale, a pellicle of being without any thickness, a message at the same time indecipherable and evident, which one has or has not received, but of which, if one has received it, one knows all there is to know, and of which in the end there is nothing to say. It requires a focusing, however brief: it emerges from a less precise, more general redness, in which my gaze was caught, into which it sank, before—as we put it so aptly—fixing it. And, now that I have fixed it, if my eyes penetrate into it, into its fixed structure, or if they start to wander round about again, the quale resumes its atmospheric existence. Its precise form is bound up with a certain wooly, metallic, or porous (?) configuration or texture, and the quale itself counts for very little compared with these participations." (P. 131).

Color is never a pellicle of being without thickness, in contradistinction to certain spectacles. Color is not deciphered without focusing, without taking into account its surroundings, the texture of the support in which it appears. A red is red in accord with or in function of its material ground, from which it cannot be separated. Also the concept of red is impossible. One could go so far as to say that it has no meaning. Color cannot be abstracted from its material ground, but it also cannot be seen except in contrast to other colors. Red is only red when it is joined with other colors which it dominates or which dominate it, which it attracts or which attract it, which it repels or which repel it. In short, it is a certain node in the weave of the simultaneous and the successive. "It is a concretion of visibility, it is not an atom." There would be no "moment" of redness? Nevertheless, color is linked to the transient much more than to other visibles. But this transience is more that of the flesh of the visible, which is recalled with difficulty, than of the precision of form (and) of the concept. Red, any color, is more in the mode of *participation* than of the solitary emergence of the concept.

"*A naked color, and in general a visible, is not a chunk of absolutely hard, indivisible being, offered all naked to a vision which could be only total or null, but is rather a sort of straits between exterior horizons and interior horizons ever gaping open.*" (P. 132).

What is perceived would be not so much the color and the thing but the difference between things and colors. Sensation would have neither an object nor a moment, but it would take place only in the intervals *between*, through difference, succession. A sort of silent scale?

Ferdinand de Saussure describes the meaning [*sens*] of language thus, at least its organization. For Merleau-Ponty, is sensation already structured like a language? There would be no place for this bath in which my gaze is immersed, nor for this contemplation which touches on eternity, or which joins the moment and eternity. The gaze on or of the flesh of the visible is still modulated in the manner of a demiurgic possession. . . . Which reverses values somewhat? Sensation is without doubt what we feel as most naively instantaneous. All the more reason to remember this, and that it is not a simple reserve for the appearance of the concept.

"*Between the alleged colors and the visible, we would find anew the tissue that lines them, sustains them, nourishes them, and which, for its part is not a thing, but a possibility, a latency, and a* flesh *of things.*" (Pp. 132–33).

Where does this tissue come from? How is it nourished? Who or what gives it consistency? My body? My flesh? Or a maternal, maternalizing flesh, reproduction, subsistence there of the amniotic, placental tissue, which enveloped subject and things prior to birth, or of tenderness and the milieu that constituted the atmosphere of the nursling, the infant, still of the adult.

Here, Merleau-Ponty makes flesh go over to the realm of things and as if to their place of emergence, their prenatal ground, their nourishing soil. . . . Indefinitely, he has exchanged seer and visible, touching and tangible, "subject" and "things" in an alternation, a fluctuation that would take place in a mileu that makes possible their passage from one or the other "side." An archaic fleshly atmosphere, a sojourn that it is difficult not to compare once again to the intrauterine or to the still barely differentiated symbiosis of infancy. Whence come *eyes*? Only eyes? But also *in the world*. Things would look at us. Above all where color or colors are concerned, things would recall all that they keep of the flesh of the world and notably of visibility.

According to Merleau-Ponty, the look would be a variant of touch. It palpates, envelops, espouses things. It discovers them as if it already knew them, "as though it knew them before knowing them." And no one knows who commands this secret complicity between things and the "subject," this "prepossession of the visible." No one knows, but the relationship of touching and being touched, which is very close to that of interrogating and being interrogated, perhaps indicates the secret of this still "obscure" alliance between looking and being looked

[*159*]

at. If my hands can quickly and with deft movement perceive the textures of matter—for example, of what is smooth or rough—this is a function of their kinship with the tactile world.

"This can happen only if my hand, while it is felt from within, is also accessible from without, itself tangible, for my other hand, for example, if it takes its place among the things it touches, is in a sense one of them, opens finally upon a tangible being of which it is also a part. Through this crisscrossing within it of the touching and the tangible, its own movements incorporate themselves into the universe they interrogate, are recorded on the same map as it." (P. 133).

This is only possible, if my hand, felt from within, is accessible from without, itself tangible to another hand. If it takes its place among the things it touches, opens onto the tangible of which it is a part, and if there occurs within it the crisscrossing of the touching and the tangible. Thus, "its own movements incorporate themselves into the universe they interrogate, are recorded on the same map as it; the two systems are applied upon one another, as the two halves of an orange" (p. 133).

My movements *incorporate* themselves in the universe they interrogate. Two introjections, introspections cross. Two passages from within to without, from without to within, would be recorded on the same map. My hand and its "other side," and the universe and its "other side" would be inscribed on the same horizon, would mingle their knowledges, their assimilations, in the same cycle or orbit, each one putting the other within-without, without-within? Which is impossible? Neither my hand nor the world is a "glove," nor can either be reduced to its clothing. Neither my hand nor the world is thus reversible. They are not pure actual phenomena, pure pellicles that are graspable one by the other, even empathetically. They have their roots, which are not reducible to the visible moment. Their roots and their atmospheres. To reverse them thus, the one in the other, would amount to destroying them in their own lives.

My hand feels itself from within and it is felt from without.

These two "systems are applied opon one another, as the two halves of an orange. It is no different for the vision."

This comparison with the orange seems strange. Is it still "valid," if the *two hands* are *joined*? Which brings about something very particular in the relation feeling-felt. With no object or subject. With no passive or active, or even middle-passive. A sort of fourth mode? Neither active, nor passive, nor middle-passive. Always more passive than the passive. And nevertheless active. The hands joined, palms together, fingers outstretched, constitute a very particular touching. A gesture often reserved for women (at least in the West) and which evokes, doubles, the *touching of the lips* silently applied upon one another. A touching more intimate than that of one hand taking hold of the other. A phenomenology of the passage between interior and exterior. A phenomenon that remains in the interior, does not appear in the light of day, speaks of itself only in gestures, remains always on the edge of speech, gathering the edges without sealing them. This gesture, reserved for prayer (?), could represent that of the two halves of the universe applied one upon the other at different times of their becoming. It can also be performed with the gaze: the eyes meet in a sort of silence of vision, a screen of resting before and after seeing, a reserve for new landscapes, new lights, a punctuation in which the eyes reconstitute for themselves the frame, the screen, the horizon of a vision.

"There is double and crossed situating of the visible in the tangible and of the tangible in the visible; the two maps are complete, and yet they do not merge into one. The two parts are total parts and yet are not superposable." (P. 134).

Of course there is a relation of the visible and the tangible. Is the doubling redoubled and crisscrossed? This is less certain. The look cannot take up the tangible. Thus I never see that *in which* I touch or am touched. What is at play in the caress does not see itself. The in-between, the middle, the *medium* of the caress does not see itself. In the same way and differently, I do not see that which allows me to see, that which touches me with light and air so that I see some "thing." This is perhaps, as far as I am concerned, what Merleau-Ponty calls the site of flesh in which things bathe? They begin to appear in a fog or a mist of invisibility. And it is still possible that my look—the most developed of all the senses?—disturbs the intelligence of my hand, of my touching. That it makes a screen which freezes the tactile nuptials, paralyzing the flow, turning it to ice, precipitating it, undoing its rhythm. The visible and the tactile do not obey the same laws or rhythms of the flesh. And if I can no doubt unite their powers, I cannot reduce the one to the other. I cannot situate the visible and the tangible in a chiasmus. Perhaps the visible needs the tangible but this need is not reciprocal?

Besides, if this doubled and crisscrossed situating of which Merleau-Ponty speaks neglects the sensible *medium*, then it also neglects the *mucous* of the carnal. We can agree that there is a situating of the visible in the tangible and of the tangible in the visible. But the two maps are incomplete and do not overlap: *the tangible is, and remains, primary in its opening.* Its touching on, of, and by means of the other. The dereliction of its ever touching this first touching. Which is true of the visible. And which opens up the question of "God" but in a certain forgetfulness of the primary maternal-feminine. Which entails the fact that God is always entrusted to the look and never sufficiently imagined as tactile bliss. Who imagines the beyond as an infinitely blissful touching? Being touched by God, for example. Which is impossible to imagine insofar as God is the counterweight to immersion in intrauterine touching?

Deprived of this bliss, God will always be thought of as a god who touches in suffering but not in joy or bliss. A God who wounds in order to reopen the way to primary nostalgia? Never a God who envelops me, surrounds me, cradles me. . . . Who loves me carnally, erotically. Why not? What kind of God is this? One who corresponds to a transcendental that is metaphysical but not physical (except prior to the first sin?). A God who would have created me as man or woman to make me guilty of my *body*? Who would have made us male and female to make the fulfillment of his creation sinful, forbidden, or impossible? Who is this God? And who has, since the beginning, commited the sin of simony vis-à-vis God? While speculating on the text of the law? But above all while exploiting (consciously or unconsciously) the meaning of the word. This is a difficult question; but more and more it seems to me that God has always been a victim of simony. Were it otherwise, would grace come to pass more easily? Whoever writes a truth or makes a pronouncement, above all concerning God, should always add: *open* [*ouvert(e)*].

Thus there is a crossing of the tangible in the visible and of the visible in the tangible, according to Merleau-Ponty. In this situating can be understood a desire for mastery that denies the opening of each of the maps.

But,

— I do not see the source of light that allows me to see. I sense it, often when I forget about it.

— I do not see the sound source that allows me to hear; I sense it.

— I do not see my body, or only a little.

— I do not see that *in which* I caress; the caress always takes place in a milieu which is its "proper" milieu, which remains invisible; the most tangible of the tangible or the tangible "itself" does not see itself.

Moreover, the chiasmus of the visible and the tangible is inversed in time. Is this what is at stake in the first sin? The tangible is primary and the visible claimed to equal it, even to surpass it. A tangible should remain intangible to figure as a blank space of the tangible in the visible: thou shalt not *touch* the tree of the *knowledge* of *good* and *evil*. The fact of having *touched* the fruit of that tree, of having tasted it, turned the tangible into something forbidden (you shall not touch each other, except to reproduce), and especially in the flesh of the visible: they saw that they were naked and they were obliged to cover themselves. The tangible represented a divine happiness, an "earthly paradise," until the moment when it entered into the perspective of the knowledge of good and evil. Of black and white? Of dichotomous oppositions that break into its tissue, riddle it with judgments, that transform touch into something other than itself while destroying palpation in disembodied, abstract forms of the sensible, cutting it up according to alternatives that respect neither its thresholds, its approaches, nor its mouths.

What is more, this transgression of the limits of the flesh, and of its visible, to have access to knowledge, or another knowledge, resulted in exile from the threshold of the earthly paradise, where the door of the garden and the entryways of the flesh overlapped according to the destiny that God had given us. For having wanted access to a knowledge that was alienated from carnal happiness, a knowledge that situated the tangible in the visible and the visible in the tangible according to the usual mode of our *episteme*, man was condemned to labor, suffering, carnal exile, the quest for God, the exploitation of nature for his nourishment. . . .

The two maps of the visible and the tangible are not completely situated the one in the other and the other in the one. If one were to "situate" [*relever*], it would be the tangible. But it remains instead the ground that is available for all the senses. A landscape much vaster but never enclosed in a map, the tangible is the matter and memory for all of the sensible. Which remembers without remembering thematically? It constitutes the very flesh of all things that will be sculpted, sketched, painted, felt, and so on, out of it.

First of all, the tangible is received, perceived prior to the dichotomies of active and passive. It is received like a bath that affects without and within, in fluidity. It is never completely situated in the visible. And, furthermore, in the tangible itself, it is not sure that it can transform itself into act.

With regard to the look, perhaps it is acquired later, even

though it is received from and in the flesh, and it would or could take up that which can not be taken up? Can I live in the visible independent of touch? I can certainly go quite far. I distance myself, for the greater part, from my sensible body. And it remains that I see only by the touch of the light, and my eyes are situated in my body. I am touched and enveloped by the felt even before seeing it.

The question is perhaps that of the "situating" or of the translation into my interior landscape. It is the felt that should conduct me there. Can I transform, transmute the sensible into some inwardness? How so? What will be lacking from this intimate landscape? It will always be incomplete.

With regard to the movements of my eyes, they do not take place uniquely within the visible universe: they also happen in the living crypt of my body and my flesh.

"*Without even entering into the implications proper to the seer and the visible, we know that, since vision is a palpation with the look, it must also be inscribed in the order of being that it discloses to us; he who looks must not himself be foreign to the world that he looks at. As soon as I see, it is necessary that the vision (as is so well indicated by the double meaning of the word) be doubled with a complementary vision or with another vision.*" (P. 134).

Someone must see me, so that I can be possessed by whoever sees me.

Without examining how far this identity of the seer and the visible may go, two questions can be put to him:

— that of the *prenatal sojourn* which is always invisible, in any case to my eyes, and in a way that another seer can see me seeing and I can see him: in this sense none of us can be substituted for his (or her) mother from the perspective of the gaze, the daughter being able to palpate the invisible "as" her mother does (the "as" is meaningful only through its difference from the impossibility of one who never carries an infant in her womb);

— that of the place of an *other sex* which sees me without

[*165*]

my being able to see it too, and vice versa, especially in the name of the tangible and of an irreversible inversion of the gaze into a flesh for which no other can be substituted.

"The body unites us directly with things through its own ontogenesis, by welding to one another the two outlines of which it is made, its two lips: the sensible mass it is and the mass of the sensible where it is born by segregation and upon which, as seer, it remains open." (P. 136; translation modified).[2]

Two lips, a strange comparison: one on its side (the sensible mass it is), one on the side of the other (mass where it is born through segregation), to which, as a *seer*, it remains open. One lip that remains in or of its own sensible, another from which it will emerge, which it will see, and to which it will stay tied as seer. One that remains more on the side of touch? The other with the flesh of the visible? Two lips that do not touch each other in the same sensible realm, that, rigorously speaking, do not touch at all, unlike the lips of our "body."

The singularity of the body and the flesh of the feminine comes:

— both from the fact that the lips are doubled there: those above and those below;

— and from the fact that the sensible which is the feminine touches the sensible from which he or she emerges. The woman being woman and potentially mother, the two lips of which Merleau-Ponty speaks can touch themselves in her, between women, without having recourse to seeing. These two dimensions of which Merleau-Ponty speaks are *in* her body. And hence she experiences it as volume in a different way?

[2] (At this point in Lingis's English translation, "laps" is substituted for "lips," a typographical error that seems to mime what Irigaray calls the invisibility of the feminine.—Tr.)

And this would be one of the differences between men and women, that these lips do not re-join each other according to the same economy. Whereas one needs the mother or her substitute, the other suffices within herself to be two, being mother and woman. The two being in the same already and still in the invisible?

"Ideas are the other side of language and calculus. When I think they animate my interior speech, they haunt it as the 'little phrase' possesses the violinist, and they remain beyond the words as it remains beyond the notes—not in the sense that under the light of another sun hidden from us they would shine forth but because they are that certain divergence, that never-finished differentiation, that openness ever to be reopened between the sign and the sign, as the flesh is, we said, the dehiscence of the seer into the visible and of the visible into the seer." (P. 153; translation modified).

This never-finished differentiation might be the symptom, the secret recollection of a sexual difference that has never been achieved in language. Something would always sing "behind" words, like the trace of the resistance of an other that is irreducible to myself, that would require the unceasing practice of openness between signs. Letting the flesh appear between the sign and the sign. Dehiscence of the seer in the visible and of the visible in the seer which is insurmountable between these two "signs": masculine and feminine, living signs that, as seer and visible, will never see each other. That in which their differences consist is experienced in touch but is never "seen." Not even in the meeting of their flesh. Flesh, the flesh of each one is not substitutable for the other. It is—prior to any God—transcendence here and now. While God can help to arrange space, space-time, he never takes "the place of." He lets difference be achieved, even invites it to happen. He does not fulfill it.

An Ethics of Sexual Difference

"And just as my body sees only because it is a part of the visible in which it opens forth, the sense upon which the arrangement of the sounds opens reflects back upon that arrangement." (Pp. 153–54).

"My body sees only because it is part of the visible." If I cannot see the other in his alterity, and if he cannot see me, my body no longer sees anything in difference. I become blind as soon as it is a question of a differently sexed body. I may barely perceive some exterior phenomenon that reveals a little of the flesh of the visible. Where this is concerned, I remain in darkness, operating on "premonitions," "tact," "radar," "wavelengths"? And the abundance of vestimentary compensation [*suppléance*] hardly makes up for this nudity, this dereliction? of my sexed body, devoid of carnal visibility.

Not seeing that *"because it is part of the visible in which it opens forth, the sense upon which the arrangement of the sounds opens"* reflects back on my body.

In utero, I see nothing (except darkness?), but I hear. Music comes before meaning. A sort of preliminary to meaning, coming after warmth, moisture, softness, kinesthesia. Do I hear first of all? After touch. But I cannot hear without touching; nor see, moreover. I hear, and what I hear is sexually differentiated. Voice is differentiated.

Do meaning and language inverse the order of hearing? Thus, first of all, I hear something of the feminine, some vocalizing in the feminine. However, language is said, is ordered in the masculine, except when it is a case of what linguists call a mark. The feminine follows the masculine grammatical norm, which is supposedly neuter or neutral, by adding to it a mark: *e*.[3] The feminine precedes and follows the masculine in language. The first music and the first meaning are perceived differently from what will or will not result from them as felt. Only rarely does the first music return to the subject (cf. Nietzsche's nostalgia on

[3] (In French, an *e* is the mark of feminine gender.—Tr.)

this subject, for example). When meaning does return, it is normally marked "grave," in the different senses of the word, while the first music is on the light, acute side. This vocalism is the most memorable, and/but it is not repeated in the weave of language. Which would come into being to take its place?

"For the linguist language is an ideal system, a fragment of the intelligible world." (P. 154).
Language is an ideal system not only for the linguist but for every speaking subject. In our language, we are always basically idealists. Cut off from mother nature, where, whence, we are born, from our archaic state, our archives of flesh. Twisted "upon ourselves," but starting from a primary part of the self that is abandoned "with the other"—another feminine for both sexes. A part of the self does not come back to us in its primary-perception-reception. A part of our vitality that is buried, forgotten with the other, sometimes in the other, and which we receive with an other "voice," that of an ideal order (?) which covers us over. And which lacks voice, moreover. The text of the law, of codes, no longer has a voice. Even if it is in some way built upon the "model" of the voice.

"But, just as for me to see it is not enough that my look be visible for X, it is necessary that it be visible for itself, through a sort of torsion, reversal, or specular phenomenon, which is given from the sole fact that I am born." (P. 154).
Why does birth imply this solipsism? It is true that it implies solitude. But can solitude be represented as this "torsion on oneself," notably through a specular phenomenon? Do the specular and the carnal belong to the same or to different orders? How do they articulate with each other, exclude each other? And, even though I can touch myself in a number of parts of my body, it is not possible for me to see myself in some of these. Notably it is impossible for me to see my look. I can see myself, partially, by narrowing my field of vision. I see certain parts of

my body. But my *face* is never visible to me—naturally. I need a mirror to see it, and I never see it during the activities that constitute its carnal visibility. Does my face represent what is at stake in the passage from nature to culture, the stakes of representation? My back is difficult for me to see as well. And I am always being veiled, unveiled, violated by the other in this face. And the parts of my body that I cannot protect from my look.

Nor will I ever see the *mucous*, that most intimate interior of my flesh, neither the touch of the outside of the skin of my fingers nor the perception of the inside of these same fingers, but another threshold of the passage from outside to inside, from inside to outside, between inside and outside, between outside and inside: I will always feel veiled, unveiled, violated, often by the other in this dimension which I cannot protect with my look. These mucous membranes evade my mastery, just as my face does, yet differently. The joined hands, not those that take hold one of the other, grasp each other, but the hands that touch without taking hold—like the lips. The joined hands perhaps represent this memory of the intimacy of the mucous.

As for mirrors, they give access to another order of the visible. Cold, icy, frozen-freezing, and with no respect for the vital, operative qualities of laterality. I see myself in the mirror as if I were an other. I put that other that I am in the mirror between the other and myself, which disconcerts this experience of the inversed laterality of the other. The other whose left hand can seize my right hand, for example. Making me more passive than any passivity of and within my own touch. Forcing me into the within and the beyond of my horizon. Of all possible mastery. Whether it's an event or an accident, that depends. . . . Between the other in the mirror and the other who inverts me, there is also the other of the same, at once closer and more distant. Also a phenomenon of visibility, given that without realizing it, the other detains my look as it sees him, and that he sees that which I cannot see of myself. A mutual dereliction in which we constitute, each for the other, holes in the invisible other than intra-uterine life or carnal relations in the strict sense. The black hole of that into which we disappear, each into the other, continually.

Traditionally, man claims to be the one who sees, the one whose horizon would not be pierced from one end to the other both by his "own" vision and by the look of the other who sees him. This belief, this will for mastery, probably constitutes one of the the most fundamental illusions of the flesh. The screen or armor that places an interdiction on loving relations. And the postulate of a God who is both invisible and who sees all, which makes up for the blind gaze of the other.

My face is always in darkness. It is never born. This is proba-bly why it is at stake in a metaphysics that wants to bring into the light that which is not yet clear. And that maintains the most radical *polemos* with the maternal, the intrauterine: irreducible darkness.

(It is odd that when Jacques Lacan theorized the entrance into the specular world, he described the infant and its mother seeing themselves and each other in the same mirror. If the infant does not see himself alone in the mirror, how can he differentiate himself from his mother? He runs the risk of reduplicating, or creating, a confusing fusion with her if he enters into this other world with her.

Moreover, it does not seem that he needs a mirror to look at his mother and perceive her as *you*. The mirror functions as the sword of differentiation, the passage to a world other than that of the living, but not as that which would give the child access to the way out of the mother's world. To affirm this would be to say that he lacks the ability to use his eyes, including as a mirror, and that he needs a mirror to see the other.)

"So also, if my words have a meaning, it is not because they present the systematic organization the linguist will disclose, it is because that organization, like the look, refers back to itself: the operative Word is

[171]

the obscure region whence comes the instituted light, as the muted reflection of the body upon itself is what we call natural light." (P. 154).

If my words have meaning, it is because they touch the other from the starting point of my perception, and having touched me and touching the other, they organize a possible dwelling for these perceptions. When the other understands, he gives and returns to me my dwelling. So long as he or she inhabits and relates to himself or herself in a habitable way. And so long as my words carry the meaning of a dwelling. Whence comes the necessity of "organization," a sort of "house" that does not cut itself off from perceptions but shelters them and allows them to inhabit, cohabit, socially as well as politically.

"The operative Word is the obscure region whence comes the instituted light." (P. 154).

That which is operative in the word remains obscure once light is instituted. Thus light and its norms are based on an efficacy or an effectivity that is not very clear. Is the maternal-feminine engaged, enacted, while remaining in obscurity, especially where its social impact is concerned?

"As there is a reversibility of the seeing and the visible, and as at the point where the two metamorphoses cross what we call perception is born. . . ." (P. 154).

This reversibility is Merleau-Ponty's hypothesis. As if the *seen* enveloped me in its vision? Isn't this a sort of animism in which the visible becomes another living being? In his view, are the seeing and the visible two aspects of himself? Two metamorphoses of himself that intersect in a closed system? Perception takes place in this crisscrossing of the seeing and the visible, of the look and the visible, of the one who looks and the world, things that are already enveloped, surrounded, "layered" by looks. Does the seer see-perceive because of the fact that the visible is already clairvoyance? I would not be able to receive the visible world if there were no kinship between what I see there and my vision. This reversibility of the *world* and the *I* (which Merleau-Ponty refuses to dissociate, to separate into two) suggests some repetition of a prenatal sojourn where the universe and I form a closed economy, which is partly reversible (but only in the opposite direction, if reversibility can have meaning: the in utero *providing* it, the *hypokeimenon*, is more on the side of the maternal-feminine, the future "subject" or seer on the side of the world or of things), or some anticipation of a heavenly sojourn, unless it is an alliance or a love pact between the world and things. In this indivisibility of the seer in relation to the visible, does some trace of animism remain as a sort of enveloping by the maternal power that is still present following birth, or as an anticipation of the presence of God? Or both? In this idea, something is said about the fact that no mourning has been performed for the birth process, nor for the cutting of reversibility through some umbilical cord. Although a pertinent analysis of the way I form a weave of sensations with the world, it is one that excludes solitude even though its own systemization is solipsistic. This seer is never alone, he dwells unceasingly in *his* world. Eventually he finds some accomplices there, but he never meets others. His universe represents, or re-creates, a vast intertwining of umbilical cords or passages. Perception would take place at each crossing of placental tissue with an embryo-nurseling that is always in direct connection with it (her).

If I wanted to apply some terms here which I do not really like to use outside of their strictly clinical setting—where, moreover, I do not use them as such—I might say that Merleau-Ponty's seer remains in an incestuous prenatal situation with the whole. This mode of existence or of being is probably that of all men, at least in the West. Also, given the historic period when Merleau-Ponty was writing, he would have been one of the few or one of the first people to have felt this. Is it still true that the perception of this situation remains veiled, an obscure light which illuminates the whole? Still without changing the movement or the dimension of "things" or of the relations between them.

"So also there is a reversibility of the speech and what it signifies; the signification is what comes to seal, to close, to gather up the multiplicity of the physical, physiological, linguistic means of elocution, to contract them into one sole act." (P. 154).

Speech, too, would form a sort of tissue with that which it signifies, signification coming to seal up each act, a crossroads of speech acts. Like a weaving stitch that holds the threads in a given space-time, fulfills their potentialities, their powers in a realization which, for this moment, completes the work, its virtualities.

"As vision comes to complete the aesthesiological body. . . ." (P. 154).

Merleau-Ponty accords an exorbitant privilege to vision. Or else, once again, he expresses the exorbitant privileging of vision in our culture. Must my aesthesiological body be completed by vision? Why completed? Why vision? Does it represent the sense which is the most capable of completing? The most unveiling/reveiling? That which covers? Especially gaps, depths, abysses? That which finishes, finishes me in relation to the other? In particular the other who is touching and being touched. The look by which I touch also creates a spectacle that allows me to approach the other without immediately being open to his, or her, senses. At least I may think so. And think of myself as autonomous, completed by my visual construction. It becomes the power and the fault in my aesthesiological body. Equally because in a certain way nothing is as sensitive, especially to touch, as my sight. But it can give me the illusion of a closed world, one that is closed because of the fact that I, male or female, was born of, issued from, an other, woman-mother.

What Merleau-Ponty seeks is something that closes the circuit of my relations with the universe in all its dimensions, and that allows me to perceive in the place where it is closed up. Vision is effectively a sense that can totalize, enclose, in its own way. More than the other senses, it is likely to construct a landscape, a horizon. Up to a certain point. It happens that movement is a more adequate way of building myself an aesthesiological body. And that, moving through the world, across the universe, or dancing, I construct more of a dwelling for myself than through vision. Merleau-Ponty would want it to be vision which closes— and works—my body, including the reversibility of the visible. And for the horizon to perfect me in a network, a garment, a skin, which we give ourselves, which we weave unceasingly in order to live, to be born. And to dwell, also, in a certain darkness, enveloped, also, in the visible, which is never pure transparency but carries in it, with it, the opacity, the weight, the thickness of the flesh. His analysis of vision becomes even more detailed, more beautiful, as it accords him the privilege over the other senses, as it takes back a great deal of the phenomenology of the tactile. Of course, vision is a mode of the tactile, but by giving it the privilege of closing up the aesthesiological body, Merleau-Ponty says of it what he could have said of the skin, the mucous, of their contacts. His phenomenology of vision almost mistakes itself for a phenomenology of painting or of the art of painting. On occasion, he speaks of it with the lyricism of one who loves art rather than with the rigor of a philosopher, as if one must give oneself over to to its weights and measures. It is simply a question of signifying that this privilege accorded to vision indeed gives it some dimensions that metaphysics neglects, but there still remains the *privilege* of this sense over the others. Reduction of the tactile into the visible, to begin with. Fulfillment of the idea, of idealism, under its material, carnal aspects. A way of talking about the flesh that already cancels its most powerful components, those that are moreover creative in their power. At least there is a great risk of perpetuating this state of things when the relation to the world is "closed" or directed by the visible (or by that tactility between the hands which is at issue in this text).

"And, as the visible takes hold of the look which has unveiled it and which forms a part of it, the signification rebounds upon its own means, it annexes to itself the speech that becomes an object of science, it antedates itself by a retrograde movement which is never completely belied—because already, in opening the horizon of the nameable and of the sayable, the speech acknowledged that it has its place in that horizon; because no locutor speaks without making himself in advance allocutary, be it only for himself; *because with one sole gesture he closes the circuit of his relation to himself and that of his relation to the others, and, with the same stroke, also sets himself up as* delocutary, *speech of which one speaks: he offers himself and offers every word to a universal Word."* (P. 154).

Signification is in language. It antedates itself in language, the expectation of speech as well as the look in the visible. The movement (since it is a question here of aesthesiology) does not seem the same in each case. Language would be more of the order of a temporal bridge between retroaction and anticipation. The "subject" keeping itself always in this endless crisscrossing of an anticipation and a recurrence [*effet de retour*], a reversal [*effet de rebours*] to that which is said and which becomes available for another saying. There again, the circle is closed by the sedimentations of its comings and goings.

Two points may be noted, among others:

1. The circularity of these speech patterns explains why it is so difficult to effect any changes. The entire speaking body of the subject is in some way archaeologically structured by an already spoken language. To signify to him that this language must or can be modified amounts to asking him to modify body, his flesh. Which cannot be done in a day. Or in a year. Resistance to all the discoveries that convulse language can be understood in this way. Also the impossibility of accepting, without a detach-

ment that is truly difficult to conceive for one who does not feel its carnal necessity, the idea that discourse is *monosexual* and that it is necessary to make room, leave a place, for another discourse, one that is put together differently. This resistance shows itself to be at least as strong, if not stronger, where psychoanalysts are concerned, insofar as they deal with a store of conscious language. They do not accept for all that that this store, this *background*,[4] might be interpretable, might unfold itself like a language, the repressed-censored of another sex that asks to come into being.

2. These sedimentations of language weave between past and future, and my present speech is rooted in what has already been said and closes up the circularity between the subject and his speech. Language, languages find themselves constituted like another ground, or rather like another circular matrix, with which the subject maintains permanent exchanges, from which he receives himself without always being able or willing to modify it. Moreover, he calls his language his "mother tongue," which is the sign of a substitution rather than a reality. His language is in no way created by a mother or mothers, except insofar as it sometimes reduplicates the dwelling in the mother and in nature. But this reproduction is not a maternal creation.

This language and these languages, therefore, are firmly rooted, and undoubtedly there is nothing more difficult than changing their culture. Especially since the subject also anticipates his interlocutor, his allocutor, since he creates his own allocutor, since "with one sole gesture he closes the circuit of his relation to himself and that of his relation to the others, and, with the same stroke, also sets himself up as *delocutary*, speech of which one speaks: he offers himself and offers every word to a universal Word" (p. 154). In his speech acts but also in his linguistic relation with the other, the subject closes his circle, his bubble.

[4] (In English in the original text.—Tr.)

Speech is not used to communicate, to encounter, but to talk to oneself, to duplicate and reduplicate oneself, to surround, even to inter oneself. There is no becoming, except that which is already closed off. No air, except that which would exhale words already spoken, already brought into existence? Nothing new, nothing being born in this *universal word* which amounts to the most solipsistic construction, constitution of a subject who would no longer know, or not know, the event. Who, in a certain way, would always have been there, turning in circles from the beginning, in a language that has been determined in this way. Like a present that would move around while remaining the same? A sort of puncture in the tissue of the world, between the tissue of the world and that of the subject, between the tissue of language and the thread of the subject, as both are transposed and exchanged with each other, like a machine that puts or sews things together by making a forward stitch backward, a backward stitch forward, and so on, indefinitely. Without any creation, invention, event, or randomness except for this interminable operation.

No new speech is possible here. One cannot imagine any allocutor, any other of either sex. No other description tells so rigorously of incarceration in a "universal Word." This Word which would not give place to the unforeseeability of God, the universe, the other. A Word of "perpetual repetition"? A Word that no longer has an *open* future and consequently shuts out certain enunciatory practices: cries for help, announcements, demands, expressions of gratitude, prophecy, poetry, and so on. Necessarily, an other is present in these practices, but not that allocutor for whom I can substitute myself, whom I can anticipate. The circuit is open. Meaning does not function like the circularity of something already given and received. It is still in the process of making itself. And the superior overview of a metalanguage is and will always be partial where this is concerned. It is not possible to overhang or encircle such a production of speech. Ceaselessly engaged in seeking its rhythm, its measure, its poetry, its house, its country, its passages, its short-cuts, toward itself, toward the other, others—the same or foreign—its ethics. A speech that is always at risk, stable and unstable, like a step that is discovering itself, inventing itself at each instant, also in function of the newness of the landscape. A speech in which there is nothing of the universal. Even if occa-sionally it expresses the universe better than an unchanging, eternal speech. A neutral speech, about the neuter? The speech of a subject who tries unceasingly to compensate for his incarna-tion in his language, his tongue, and who elaborates moreover a technically powerful machine, a sort of mechanical miming of parturition, but one that is not a "sublimation of the flesh." Hardly even a mechanism of solipsistic survival. A kind of du-plication or stand-in for the constitution of the flesh? A reversal of the maternal gift of flesh, in the autarchy of the subject of and in language.

For a sublimation of the flesh, what is lacking is a passage through silence and solitude which leads to the existence, the emergence of a speech of one who is born in a space still to be defined by him, to be marked by him, so that, when speaking of himself, he can also speak of himself to the other, and hear him.

"We shall have to follow more closely this transition from the mute world to the speaking world. For the moment we want only to suggest that one can speak neither of a destruction nor of a conservation of silence (and still less of a destruction that conserves or of a realization that destroys—which is not to solve but to pose the problem). When the silent vision falls into speech, and when the speech in turn, opening up a field of the nameable and the sayable, inscribes intself in that field, in its place, according to its truth—in short, when it metamorphoses the structures of the visible world and makes itself a gaze of the mind, intuitus mentis—this is always in virtue of the same fundamental phenomenon of reversibility which sustains both the mute perception and the speech and which manifests itself by an almost carnal existence of the idea, as well as by a sublimation of the flesh." (Pp. 154–55).

There is no silence for Merleau-Ponty. The structure of a mute world is such that all the possibilities of language are already given there. Nothing therefore about the dereliction of the lack in language or about the creative virtualities that would inscribe themselves in this silence. Speech is or is not actualized, but its field and its means and their possible realizations are already there. Nothing new can be said. No way to say it can be invented. Everything is there and is unceasingly reversible. Just as in the case of the visible. Speech has, among other functions, that of bearing the silence of the visible into sonority, of metamorphosing it and itself into a gaze of the mind, "always in virtue of the same fundamental phenomenon of reversibility which sustains both the mute perception and the speech and which manifests itself by an almost carnal existence of the idea, as well as by a sublimation of the flesh" (p. 155).

The almost carnal existence of the idea and the sublimation of the flesh are seductive utterances and hypotheses, yet puzzling ones insofar as their permanences, their cycles or rotations are always already there, where the work that would make the idea become carnal and sublimate the flesh is never accomplished. It would be enough to remain in a state of reversibility—"the ultimate truth"—for these operations or these conditions to take place. Whereas it is the opposite. If reversibility is not interrupted, the sublimation of the flesh cannot be achieved.

In other words: if the cord is not cut and there is no end to the osmotic exchanges with the maternal world and its substitutes, how can the sublimation of the flesh take place? It keeps on becoming in a closed circuit, in a sort of nourishing relationship with the other. Is it sublimated in order to accede to union with the other? It seems that this is not the case. Does it perpetuate a condition, maintain it with its permanence, amortize its cuts and shocks? What is called reversibility here is perhaps that by means of which the subject produces some mucous on the outside and is reenveloped by it. Some elaboration of the carnal undoubtedly takes place there. But always in its solipsistic relation to the maternal. There is *no trace of any carnal idea of the other woman nor of any sublimation of the flesh with the other.* At best an alchemy of substitution of a placental nourishment. A sort of layering that represents the archaeology of the subject, of the world, of their exchanges. But this archaeology already existed. The subject and the world would be already completed even when they were engaged in making themselves. Would they elaborate themselves in relation to an unchanging ground and horizon? In order to change the subject, his language, his world, everything would have to be undone and remade, including what is called the possibilities of language. Its grounds and foundations. And this postulate of a universal speech in which we exchanged, as in some unchanging, pregiven, presupposed exchange, would have to be brought into question.

"*In a sense, if we were to make completely explicit the architectonics of the human body, its ontological framework, and how it sees itself and hears itself, we would see that the structure of its mute world is such that all the possibilities of language are already given in it. Already our existence as seers (that is, we said, as beings who turn the world back upon itself and who pass over to the other side, who see one another with eyes).*" (P. 155).

In Merleau-Ponty's view, the world turns back on itself. The seer does not open his eyes to the world or the other in a contemplation that seeks and respects their different horizons. Does he turn over the world as he turns his hand, his plaything, his creation? Could he plumb the structure of the world to its depths or manage to encompass it? But what gesture, what quality of gesture could make him believe that he has encompassed the world? Is it an intuition or a belief that Merleau-Ponty needs in order to think? A ground that he must give himself? A ground or thought that circles back to the same point while it progresses. In order to progress. Like the sun of the earth moving around the sun and around itself? We would perceive, encounter the world, look at the other at the crossing-points of these circles? Catching sight of each other, seeing each through the other.

Catching sight of each other, if we find ourselves on the course at the crisscrossing of the circles that make this possible? Which does not seem to be a matter of course given the reversibility between the visible and the seer, the closed world that reversibility entails for the *I* or the *you*. Within this world, movement is such that it would take extraordinary luck for two seers to catch sight of each other, find each other on the track of the same circle and cross paths, or look at each other as they walk in parallel lines. Or might it happen that they see each other's eyes? Another possibility which is highly unlikely. For this to come about, it would have to happen that two *seers* assimilated the "universal Word," its effects, the world, in exactly the same way, and that they found each other at the same point in space and time. An unlikely stroke of luck or chance? Or of grace? Which makes us identical at a given moment.

But Merleau-Ponty does not speak of this. The rest can only be an illusion of the flesh. We never catch sight of each other, and we do not see each other's eyes. No matter how universal speech may be, a world, *our* world separates us, a world from which we are never separated—in any case according to the kind of relations we entertain in Merleau-Ponty's analysis. We "turn the world back on itself" and "pass over to the other side" because we are seers? Undoubtedly, at each instant, for a pellicle of the horizon of visibility, not for the whole world. The world would have to be completed. Which is possible if the explanation of the architectonics of the body, "its ontological framework," shows that all the possibilities of language are given in the mute world. The world cannot be perceived without language, yet all of language exists virtually in silence. All that remains to be said is that the world is isomorphic with the subject and vice versa, and the whole is sealed up in a circle. Nothing new happens, only this permanent weaving between the world and the subject. Which supposes that the subject sees the whole, that he is the clairvoyant seeing of everything, with nothing left over—neither of the world nor of himself. If all of language already resides in the silence of the subject and of the world, like their ontological tissue, then I can turn the world back on itself and return to myself after having passed to the other side. Am I playing at hoops with the world (of) language? What do I add? Or what do I take away? It is always the same. I revolve around the "center," the point of anchorage, without getting closer. I keep on repeating a gesture which perhaps digs me in, deepens me? Digs in and deepens the world? Unites us? According to Merleau-Ponty, energy plays itself out in the backward-and-forward motion of a loom. But weaving the visible and my look in this way, I could just as well say that I close them off from myself. The texture becomes increasingly tight, taking me into it, sheltering me there but imprisoning me as well.

In a certain way, this subject never enters the world. He never emerges from an osmosis that allows him to say to the other, "Who art thou?" But also, "Who am I?" What sort of event do we represent for each other when together? Irreversible events except where death is concerned. The phenomenology of the flesh that Merleau-Ponty attempts is without question(s). It has no spacing or interval for the freedom of questioning between two. No other or Other to keep the world open. No genesis. No grace. Having become a god, man works and plays with the world until it is worn out? Very carefully. But not without a certain ennui? By himself.

"And, in a sense, to understand a phrase is nothing else than to fully welcome it in its sonorous being, or, as we put it so well, to hear what it says." (P. 155).

Here, meaning is mixed with sound, the totality of the chain of what is said, which is integral in all differentiations of the verbal chain. It is given with the words for those who have ears to hear, and who are situated in a landscape overrun with words, which is henceforth but a variant of speech. Everything is given, inside and outside. It remains only to welcome, decode, interpret, and hear.

"In a sense the whole of philosophy, as Husserl says, consists in restoring a power to signify, a birth of meaning, or a wild meaning, an expression of experience by language, which in particular clarifies the special domain of language." (P. 155).

Everything is given, and yet the function of philosophy is to restore a power to signify, a birth of meaning, or a wild meaning. The question is: can this be possible for it without changing the foundations of language? Without lifting the hypothesis that *reversibility* is the final truth? A hypothesis that must be questioned and "opened up" if a meaning which has not yet been heard is to come into existence, that of a language which is sexuate and which encounters through speech and in the world a sex which is *irreducible* to it, and with which it is impossible to have relations of reversibility without remainder.

The Fecundity of the Caress:
A Reading of Levinas,
Totality and Infinity,
"Phenomenology of Eros"

On the horizon of a story is found what was in the beginning: this naive or native sense of touch, in which the subject does not yet exist. Submerged in *pathos* or *aisthesis*: astonishment, wonder, and sometimes terror before that which surrounds it.

Eros prior to any *eros* defined or framed as such. The sensual pleasure of birth into a world where the look itself remains tactile—open to the light. Still carnal. Voluptuous without knowing it. Always at the beginning and not based on the origin of a subject that sees, grows old, and dies of losing touch with the enthusiasm and innocence of a perpetual beginning. A subject already "fixed." Not "free as the wind." A subject that already knows its objects and controls its relations with the world and with others. Already closed to any initiation. Already solipsistic. In charge of a world it enjoys only through possession. With no communion and childlike acceptance of that which is given. A consumer who consumes what he produces without wonder at that which offers itself to him before any finished product occurs.

Sensual pleasure can reopen and reverse this conception and construction of the world. It can return to the evanescence of subject and object. To the lifting of all schemas by which the other is defined. Made graspable by this definition. *Eros* can arrive at that innocence which has never taken place with the other as other. At that nonregressive in-finity of empathy with the other. At that appetite of all the senses which is irreducible to any obligatory consumption or consummation. At that indefinable taste of an attraction to the other which will never be satiated. Which will always remain on the threshold, even after entering into the house. Which will remain a dwelling, preceding and following the habitation of any dwelling.

This gesture, which is always and still preliminary to and in all nuptials, which weds without consum(mat)ing, which perfects while abiding by the outlines of the other, this gesture may be called: the touch of the caress.

Prior to and following any positioning of the subject, this touch binds and unbinds two others in a flesh that is still and always untouched by mastery. Dressing the one and the other without and within, within and without in a garment that neither evokes, invokes, nor takes pleasure in the perversity of the naked but contemplates and adorns it, always for a first time, with an in-finite, un-finished flesh. Covering it, uncovering it again and again, like an amorous impregnation that seeks out and affirms otherness while protecting it.

In that place, nothing attests to the subject. The ever prolonged quest for a birth that will never take place, whose due date still and always recedes on the horizon. Life always open to what happens. To the fleeting touch of what has not yet found a setting. To the grace of a future that none can control. That will or will not happen. But while one waits for it, any possession of the world or of the other is suspended. A future coming not measured by the transcendence of death but by the call to birth of the self and the other. For which each one arranges and rearranges the environment, the body, and the cradle, without closing off any aspect of a room, a house, an identity.

The fecundity of a love whose most elementary gesture, or deed, remains the caress.

Before orality comes to be, touch is already in existence. No nourishment can compensate for the grace or work of touching. Touch makes it possible to wait, to gather strength, so that the other will return to caress and reshape, from within and from without, a flesh that is given back to itself in the gesture of love. The most subtly necessary guardian of my life is the other's flesh. Approaching and speaking to me with his hands. Bringing me back to life more intimately than any regenerative nourishment, the other's hands, these palms with which he approaches without going through me, give me back the borders of my body and call me to the remembrance of the most profound intimacy. As he caresses me, he bids me neither to disappear nor to forget but rather to remember the place where, for me, the most intimate life is held in reserve. Searching for what has not yet come into being for himself, he invites me to become what I have not yet become. To realize a birth that is still in the future. Plunging me back into the maternal womb and beyond that conception, awakening me to another birth—as a loving woman.

A birth that has never taken place, unless one remains at the stage of substitution for the father and the mother, which gestures toward an act that is radically unethical. Lacking respect for the one who gave me my body and enthusiasm for the one who gives it back to me in his amorous awakening.

When the lovers, male or female, substitute for, occupy, or possess the site of those who conceived them, they founder in the unethical, in profanation. They neither construct nor inhabit their love. Remaining in the no longer or the not yet. Sacrilegious sleepers, murderous dreamers—of the one and of the other in an unconscious state that might be the site of sensual pleasure? Sterile, if it were not for the child.

Which explains the closure, the sealing up of the society of couples: barren—if it were not for the child? And the abandonment of the beloved to the anonymity of love. To that touching vulnerability of a woman who can only be mortal. At least for him and in this place.

The caress does not seek to dominate a hostile freedom. However profaning. Transgressing the freedom of God? Sensual pleasure may be nourished by this transgression. Whence its ever-increasing avidity. Its unending deferral of its own potential? While he, the lover, is sent back to the transcendental, she, the beloved,[1] is plunged into the depths. The caress does not attain that more intimate dwelling place where something gathers itself in from a more secret consummation? In and through a mucous shelter that extends from the depths to the heights? From the most subterranean to the most celestial? A circulation from the one to the other that would happen in lovemaking?

Profanity always designates a threshold: the one where the simultaneity of what is hidden and what is revealed is in operation. The passage from mucous membrane to skin? But also, the presentiment of the first dwelling place where, now, there is no one, only the memory and expectation of amorous fecundity. No nudity brings back to light the intimacy of that first house of flesh. It is always nocturnal for a certain gaze—which wishes for clothing in order not to see that it cannot see everything?

The evanescence of the caress opens on a future that differs from an approach to the other's skin here and now. Stopping at

---

[1] (At this point, the text begins to set up the differential positioning of the lover [*amant*] as a masculine subject and the beloved [*aimée*] as his feminine object. Henceforth, whenever the effects of this positioning are emphasized, *amant* is translated as "male lover" and *amante* as "female lover"; similarly, to underscore Irigaray's point that the object position is also gendered, *aimée* will be translated as "beloved woman," and *aimé* as "beloved man" or "beloved one."—Tr.)

that point risks relegating the beloved to the realm of animality once the moment of seduction, of penetration beyond anything visible, has passed. Always alien to the intimacy of the mucous, not crossing the threshold, still remaining outside, the lover continues to caress until he founders in some abyss. He does not attain communion in the most inward locus of the feeling and the felt, where body and flesh speak to each other.

In this moment of ultimate sympathy, the feeling and the felt go so far as the vertigo of "getting in over their heads," of immersion in that which does not yet have an individualized form, until they are returned to the deepest level of elementary flux, where birth is not yet sealed up in its identity. There, every subject loses its mastery and method. The path has been neither made nor marked, unless in the call to a more distant future that is offered by and to the other in the abandonment of self. Causing the possibles to recede, thanks to an intimacy that keeps unfolding itself more and more, opening and reopening the pathway to the mystery of the other.

Thus a new birth comes about, a new dawn for the beloved. And the lover. The openness of a face which had not yet been sculpted. The bloom that comes of flowing to the depths of what nourishes it again and again. Not a mask given or attributed once and for all, but an efflorescence that detaches itself from its immersion and absorption in the night's most secret place. Not without sparkling. The light that shines there is different from the one that makes distinctions and separates too neatly.

Does this mean that the beloved—and the lover—find their positions thus reversed, from inside to outside? It does not. Rather, that together, what is most interior and what is most exterior are mutually fruitful. Prior to any procreation.

The son does not resolve the enigma of the most irreducible otherness. Of course, he is not engendered without having had his place in the crypt of the beloved's womb. Where the lover falters, and whence he returns, without any possible recognition or vision of this terrain. Does the son appear to the father as the impossible image of his act of love?

But, before the appearance of the son, the beloved's fulfillment tells him, shows him, the mystery of fecundity. Looking again at the woman he has loved, the lover may contemplate the work of fecundation. And, if the surrender of the beloved woman—and of the female lover[2]—means a childlike trust, an animal exuberance, it illuminates the aesthetics and ethics of the amorous gesture, for those who take the time to reopen their eyes.

The beloved's beauty announces the fulfillment of the flesh. She is more beautiful, or differently beautiful, when she makes love than when she parades around in all her finery. The most intimate fecundity of love, of its caress, of its transcendence of all restraints on this side of the other's threshold, is proffered in this parousia—silently. Wonder at what is reborn from the heart's depths through a new conception. She would be regenerated by returning, with him, to a time before the fixed, mortal due date of her birth? Taken back to the acceptance of her life by the lover and accompanied on this side of, and beyond, a given day of reckoning.

Prior to any procreation, the lovers bestow on each other— life. Love fecundates both of them in turn, through the genesis of their immortality. They are reborn, each for the other, in the assumption and absolution of a definitive conception. Each one welcomes the birth of the other, this task of beginning where neither she nor he has met—the original infidelity. Attentive to that weakness which neither one could have wanted, they love each other as the bodies they are. Not irremediably diminished by having been born in different times and places nor by having lived prior to their mutual union and generation.

---

[2] (Henceforth, the distinction between woman as beloved [*aimée*] and woman as lover [*amante*] receives increasing emphasis.—Tr.)

The mystery of relations between lovers is more terrible but infinitely less deadly than the destruction of submitting to sameness. Than all relationships of inclusion or penetration which bar the way to that nourishment which is more intimate than all others, which is given in the act of love.

Sameness, which quarrels about how much room it is due, occupies my flesh, demarcates and subdivides my space, lays siege to and sets up camp on my horizon—making it uninhabitable for me and inaccessible to the lover.

Porosity, and its fullest responsiveness, can occur only within difference. A porosity that moves from the inside to the outside of the body. The most profound intimacy becomes a protective veil. Turns itself into an aura that preserves the nocturnal quality of the encounter, without masks. Distance of the impenetrable in the clarity of daylight, of that which perceives but never beholds itself. Sometimes it crosses itself like a threshold, while touching and being touched by the other, but is forgotten and then recollected.

How to preserve the memory of the flesh? Above all, for what is or becomes the site that underlies what can be remembered? Place of a possible unfolding of its temporality? Burial ground of the touch that metabolizes itself in the constitution of time. Secret fold stitched into the time of the other. Eternity of the Other?

While there remains this mystery of the touch that goes beyond touching, the intention of every gesture, how can one recall this permanence? Become it as one recollects it? Make time of this source of time? Arrive at this nocturnal temporalization of touch?

Without a face? The face swallowed up by the nocturnal experience of touching, touching self and other, re-touching. Veiled by that which is situated only beyond the project. Invisible because it must defend itself unceasingly from the visible and the night. Both.

Beloved, the female lover emerges from all disguises. No longer frozen in a deadly freedom but permitted growth, which is still possible, and a face without any habits, which lets itself be seen in order to be reborn beyond what has already appeared. And in a state of imperfection, the unfinished condition of every living being.

In that place, there is no discovery to scrutinize. That which lets itself go in the most intimate touch remains invisible. Touch perceives itself but transcends the gaze. And the issue of nakedness. Touch never shows itself, not even if its precision could thus be made manifest. Reaching the other, or not. But it remains palpable flesh on this side of and beyond the visible.

Spelled out in images and photographs, a face loses the mobility of its expressions, the perpetual unfolding and becoming of the living being. Gazing at the beloved, the lover reduces her to less than nothing if this gaze is seduced by an image, if her nudity, not perceived as endlessly pulsating, becomes the site of a disguise rather than of astonishment at something that moves, unceasingly and inwardly. The beloved's vulnerability is this unguarded quality of the living, revealed in a form that is never definitive. If he thinks he leaves her like a dead body, could it be that the lover discovers in her what is terrible about the limits of nudity, or dredges up what he needs to move on to some place beyond the realm of the living?

The face, or at least a certain conception, idea, or representation of it, can be swallowed up in the act of love. A new birth, which undoes and remakes contemplation by returning to the source of all the senses—the sense of touch. There is no longer any image there, except for that of letting go and giving of self. Among other ways, with the hands. Sculpting, shaping, as if for the first time, on the first day. The beloved would be engulfed in infancy or animality only to be reborn from there as flesh reshaped inside and out. Innocent of absorption in self and of self? Encounter across a threshold that differs from the irreversible one of mortal birth. Approach, communion, and regenerating fecundation of the flesh that touches itself on an ever more distant horizon, repeating and transcending the original conception.

Also surpassing the corruption of what has already been seen. Return to a certain night whence the lovers can arise differently illuminated and enlightened. They give themselves to each other and give up what has already been made. Of themselves and of reason. Opening to an innocence that runs the risk of folding back on itself in defense of the past. In this gesture, each one runs the risk of annihilating, killing, or resuscitating.

Lovers' faces live not only in the face but in the whole body. A form that is expressed in and through their entire stature. In its appearance, its touch. A *morphé* in continual gestation. Movements ceaselessly reshaping this incarnation.

The lovers meet in one moment of this incarnation. Like sculptors who are going to introduce themselves, entrust themselves to one another for a new delivery into the world.

And all the senses share in the nature of the caress, the hand serving, in its way, as the most intimate means of approach.

There the female lover is not subjected to alternations of fire and ice—mirror or frost that the male lover would have to pass through to reach the beloved. Given back to her own movements, to the demonstration of her charms, the female lover also

[*193*]

revives herself in the flame and does not simply receive it from the other. Waiting without becoming rigid, she does not close herself off or enclose herself in some sepulchre of images or some project that denies her dynamism. She tends toward her own fulfillment, already unfolds herself to gather in more.

Thus, neither the one nor the other will take the initiative of plucking the bloom in order to contemplate it. Both contemplate and bloom. Opening and closing themselves in order to keep giving each other that which they could never have brought to life. Regenerating, renewing each other, in memory and in anticipation of the moment of their mutual fecundation. Each one moving along the path to some in-finite which trembles in the encounter without closing itself up or making decisions according to the limiting dimensions of some transcendental value to be attained.

The beloved woman falls back into infancy or beyond, while the male lover rises up to the greatest heights. Impossible match. Chain of links connecting, from one end to the other, a movement of ascent in which neither is wed, except in the inversion of their reflections.

When the male lover loses himself in the depths of the beloved woman's sensual pleasure, he dwells within her as in an abyss, an unfathomable depth. Both of them are lost, each in the other, on the wrong side, or the other side, of transcendence.

Beloved woman. Not female lover. Necessarily an object, not a subject with a relation, like his, to time. She drags the male lover into the abyss so that, from these nocturnal depths, he may be carried off into an absolute future.

The beloved woman sinks into the abyss, founders in a night more primeval than the night, or finds herself dispersed in the shards of a broken mirror. Do the pearls of ice or frost of her reflection put up a screen to love? Made from the brilliance of her finery? Of the beloved man, desired in and through her, who banishes her from the place of greatest tenderness. Calling her to freeze into the shapes that separate her from herself. She who is deprived of the suppleness of her loving mobility, torn away from her source of respiration, which is also cosmic, where she moves in harmony with the fecundity of nature. For her, a living mirror. Tuned differently to the rhythm of the earth and the stars. Intimately tied to universal circulation and vibration that go beyond any enclosure within reproduction. Turning in a cycle that never resolves back to sameness. Continual and patient engendering of an obscure labor. More passive than any voluntary passivity, yet not foreign to the act of creating/procreating the world. Within her something takes place, between earth and sky, in which she participates as in a continual gestation, a mystery yet to be deciphered. Heavy with her destiny.

When the lover relegates her to the realms of infancy, animality, or maternity, one aspect of this mystery, the relation to the cosmos, is not brought to light. What is left out is participation in the construction of a world that does not forget natural generation and the human being's role in safeguarding its efflorescence. A gestation in which the subject as microcosm is not given to nourishing, sheltering, and fecundating itself at the expense of a macrocosm for which it no longer shows any concern, believing that it is given once and for all, to be exploited endlessly, carelessly, irretrievably. Cultivating one's already enclosed garden. The work of a landowner who shows no regard for the natural world that makes fecundity possible, or for the God's concern with this universe of incarnation and the harmony of its attractions.

Separating her off into the subterranean, the submarine, stone and airborne flight lacking the sparkle of light and fire. Dismissing her to a perpetual future. Forgetting that which is already insistent here and now—already hidden or still buried. Uprooting the female lover from her fundamental habitat.

Annexing the other, in all his/her dimensions and directions, in order to capture him/her, captivate him/her within a language that possesses as its principal and internal resources only the consummation and speed of its contradictions. Deployment of a network that takes in the whole and deprives it of its most intimate breath and growth. A garment that first and foremost paralyzes the other's movement. Protecting it, like the shield of the hero who defends the beloved woman from some conquering rival?

But thus shielded, how does one live ? For the woman who is so protected, what future remains? Inside this male territory, even if she plays at disguising herself in various showy and coquettish poses which he "strips away" in the act of love, she still lacks both the identity and the passport she needs to traverse or transgress the male lover's language. Is she some more or less domesticated child or animal that clothes itself in or takes on a semblance of humanity? Takes on the subject's unconscious and involuntary movements, veils them in softness, in folds, in spaciousness to give him back some room. Wraps herself up in the remainder of what he has taken in and from love. But what of her own call to the divine?

About this he has little to say. And since it is not her place to speak when he renders her profane in sensual pleasure, is he not also sacrilegious vis-à-vis God? The "God" of lightness, of "incarnation," the God of life—of the air, of blood, and of the maternity of the son who appears in the "form" of the cloud that accompanies the tablets of the law. The male lover would take this God into his discourse and beyond, refusing him the freedom of some future manifestation. He invokes this God but does not perceive him in the here and now, where God is already to be found and lost: in the sensibility of the female lover. In the creation that she perpetuates while preserving her intimacy, her inviolability, her virginity. God of the universe, God of the fecundity of a future coming, which is also preserved in the female lover.

When he does not reduce, or seduce, her to his needs, the male lover also summons her to God. This is just as regressive. Is she like a child or an animal in his eyes? Irresponsible, so that he can regain his freedom.

The very lightness of loving gestures and deeds makes one forget that when the female lover is also beloved, her abandon is inspired by the most absolute trust in the transcendence of life. Still in the future, always being reborn. Allowing herself to sink into the night, she calls forth from there a new morning, a new spring, a new dawn. The creation of a new day? From the source of a light that precedes and surpasses the limits of reason.

The first act of creation of the God? Before peopling the sky and the earth. Illumination that precedes any part in the organization, the ordering of a world. Contemplation prior to any vision. Opening to that less-than-nothing which is not nothing—light. Ultimate incorporation of the newborn man. The first discovery outside the womb, or in regeneration. The matter without which no creation of form is possible, light is the chance for emergence out of chaos and formlessness.

Returning to the depth of night, the female lover waits for light—the light that shines through discourse, that filters through words, that bestows a sense of the cosmos, but also that which is illuminated in the grace of regeneration and transfiguration? Giving herself to nature to be reborn from there, made fertile—within herself. Pregnant with a son, perhaps (but why a son and not a daughter, her other self?), but also with herself, by him. Fecundity of a love that gives itself over, on this side of and beyond reason—to the source of light. There where things have not yet taken their places but remain possible. In the future. Still germinating, growing, being revealed. The female lover will have to cultivate the intimacy (the seed?) of this fecundity and the path from the most hidden part of the night to the efflorescence of the day.

When the beloved woman presents herself or appears to the male lover as a paradise to be referred back to infancy and animality, then the act of love leads not only to profaning, but also to a destruction, a fall. The beloved woman would be cast down to the depths so that the male lover could be raised to the heights. The act of love would amount to reaching the inordinate limits of discourse, so that the woman is sent back to the position of fallen animal or child, and man to ecstasy in God. Two poles that are indefinitely separate. But perhaps the beloved woman's secret is that she knows, without knowing, that these two extremes are intimately connected.

Beneath her veils, she keeps secret watch over a threshold. A slight opening onto the depths or abysses of all language, birth, and generation. It is up to the male lover to find there or to perceive the fall into amorphousness or the astonishment of what has not yet been given form or revealed from above. To bring about *with* her, and not through or in spite of her, the assumption of the flesh. Instead of leaving her to her own profanation and despoiling, to reconstitute again and again only her virginity. To re-envelop herself in a *something more than* all humanity? Whereas the male lover leads her back to the *not yet* of the child, the *never like him* of the animal—outside human destiny. Separating himself from her with this gesture, to return to his "ethical responsibilities."

In this sense, the beloved woman, she who renounces her responsibility as a lover, succumbs to the temptation of being seduced by the male lover. She divests herself of her own will to love in order to become what is required for his exercise of will. Which assigns her to the place of nonwilling in his ethics. Her fall into the identity of the beloved one cancels out any real giving of self and makes her into a thing, or something other than the woman that she needs to be. She lets herself be taken but does not give herself. She quits the locus of all responsibility, her own ethical site. She is placed under house arrest, lacking the will and movements of love. Except for the waiting and the healing of profanation? Falling into the depths? She gathers round herself and wraps herself with what was secretly entrusted to her—without his knowledge. Barely moves at all, but unfolds round herself the garments of protection and display. Of paralysis where dance is concerned, even running the risk of resigning from the creative part of love, except for remaining desirable, guarding the source and secret of her appeal. With no responsibility for bringing to life that something more than man's strategy of seduction which lies hidden within him? For unveiling a difference that remains obscurely connected to him.

If she comes back to herself, to herself within herself, to him within herself, she may feel responsible for another parousia. She may need to create, engender, give birth to the mystery she bears—prior to any conception of a child. No longer standing in the shadow of the one who draws on the mystery, taking charge—she herself—of bringing it to light. Engendering some love prior to, as something more than, a son. And a daughter.

Generating the dwelling, her site, with the male lover. Remaining on the threshold that is always receding and in the future of a mystery she must reveal under pain of ethical dereliction? The lover would assist her in this parturition, provided he does not simply send her back to the depths. The one for the other, messengers of a future that is still to be built and contemplated. The one for the other, already known and still unknown. The one for the other, mediators of a secret, a force, and an order that also touches on the divine.

Occasionally going their separate ways, meeting again, linking up again, in order not to lose their attentiveness to what transcends their already actual becoming. Listening to what has never taken place or found its place yet, to what calls to be born.

This simultaneity of desire and transcendence is traditionally represented by the angel—the divine messenger. Who is not foreign to desire and anger in some dimension that would not be one of need.

But here, sensual pleasure would hold fast to the fate of an exorbitant ultramateriality that has fallen away from discourse. That has never been brought to fruition or fulfilled in its transcendence. Captive of a destiny, without remission. Of an original sin without possible redemption? Manifesting itself outside language, outside and in spite of reason. Beyond all measures.

For the male lover, the transcendence of the Other justifies this infidelity to love. Returning to his God in a discontinuity of *eros*. If it were not for pardon.

And what of the female lover? Grace for what has not yet gone far enough into the future or been faithful enough to the moment, for what remains unfinished, left over. Remission of deprivation, of the distress of waiting, which punctuates the chronology of the lovers' unions and separations. Both fulfilling the cycles of their solitude to come back to the other, wounded perhaps, but free for a possible return because of the pardon that each gives. Allowing each to become detached from self and from the other. Renewal of the attraction that is also nourished in the suspense of reconciliation. There, sacrifice is neither sacrifice of nor mourning for the one or the other but absolution for what was not perfect. A marker in time that opens on to infinity, without sending it back to an origin or a goal deprived of an access, a threshold.

The flesh of the rose petal—sensation of the mucous regenerated. Somewhere between blood, sap, and the not yet of efflorescence. Joyous mourning for the winter past. New baptism of springtime. Return to the possible of intimacy, its fecundity, and fecundation.

But time enters in. Too closely connected with counting and

with what has already been. And how can an evil that has lasted for such a long time be repaired in a second? Call to the other from a starting point of virginity, without any trace of scars, marks of pain, and self-enclosure? Love the other above and beyond any work of healing.

And when others continually interfere with this expectation of union, what can be done to maintain a candor that neither cries out for remission nor burdens the male lover with the task of healing wounds?

But doesn't the male lover keep asking the beloved woman to efface an original wound of which she would be the bearer? The suffering of an open body that cannot be clothed with herself, within herself, unless the lover is united with her in the joy—not the sacrifice—of the mucous, the most intimate part of the dwelling. Where crossing the threshold is no longer a profanation of the temple but an entrance into another, more secret, space. Where the female lover receives and offers the possibility of nuptials. Rapture unlike that of the conqueror who captures and dominates his prey. Rapture of return to the garden of innocence, where love does not yet know, or no longer knows, nudity as profane. Where the gaze is still innocent of the limits set by reason, of the division into day and night, the alternation of the seasons, animal cruelty, the necessity of protecting oneself from the other and from the God. Face to face encounter of two naked lovers in a nudity that is more ancient than and foreign to sacrilege. That cannot be perceived as profanation. The threshold of the garden, a welcoming cosmic home, remains open. There is no guard but love itself, innocent of the knowledge of display and of the fall.

Intuition without a goal, intuition that does not mark out but inscribes itself in an already insistent field. A prehensive intuition, which inhales from the air something of what is already there to come back to itself?

The beloved woman would be she who keeps herself available

in this way. Offering to the other what he can put to his own use? Opening the path of his return to himself, of his open future? Giving him back time?

When the beloved woman perceives the male lover in this way, does she inscribe herself in a moment of her own trajectory as he arrives at a moment of his own? He believes that she is drawing him down into the depths; she believes that he is cutting himself off from her to constitute his transcendence. Their paths cross but achieve neither an alliance nor a mutual fecundation. Except for the male lover, whose double is—the son.

The beloved woman is relegated to an inwardness that is not one because it is abyssal, animal, infantile, prenuptial, while the lover is left a solitary call to his God. Withdrawn to the opposite poles of life, they do not marry. They occupy the contrapuntal sites of human becoming. The one watches over the substrate of the elementary, of generation, but the act of love scatters her among the archaic elements of earth, sea, and airborne flight. Caressing her to reach the infinity of her center, the male lover strips or divests her of her tactility—a porosity that opens onto the universe—and consigns her to a regression of her womanly becoming, which is always in the future. He is forgetful of the fecundity, here and now, of lovemaking: the gift to each of the lovers of sexuate birth and rebirth.

The one who takes the other into the self during lovemaking is inordinately cut off by this act. There is no opportunity to mourn an impossible identification. Attraction in union, and the chance of its fecundity.

Revealed only in the son, fecundity continues to disguise itself as the fecundation of the lovers in difference. As the fruit of communion between lovers, male and female, the son becomes the male lover's ornament and display of the same as himself, the position of his identity in relation to, and through, paternity.

If conceived in this way, the son does not appear as love's fulfillment. Perhaps he bars the way to its mystery? The aspect of fecundity that is vouched for only in the son obliterates the secret of difference. As the male lover's means of return to himself outside himself, the son closes the circle: the path of a solitary ethics that, for its own need, lacking the fulfillment of nuptials, will have intersected with the female lover who fails to take responsibility—the beloved.

When recognized only in the son, love and sensual pleasure bespeak the male lover's vulnerability on the threshold of difference. His retreat and appeal to his genealogy, his future as a man, his horizon, society, and security. Turning around in a world that remains his own. Contained within and by himself, with no dwelling for the female lover, except for the shelter she gives to the son—before his birth.

If the male lover needs to prove himself in sensual pleasure, he does so in order to sink down into the other of himself. To put down the night side of himself, which he covers up in the reasonable habitat of his life and from which he gains, as he emerges, the form of his highest ascension. The body of the beloved, male or female, which has been approached through caresses, is abandoned on the threshold of the nuptials. There is no union. The seduction of the beloved woman serves as a bridge between the Father and the son. Through her, who is only an aspect of himself, the male lover goes beyond love and pleasure toward the ethical.

"In this frailty as in the dawn rises the Beloved One, who is the Beloved Woman [*l'Aimé qui est Aimée*]. An epiphany of the Beloved, the feminine is not added to an object and a Thou antecedently given or encountered in the neuter (the sole gender formal logic knows). The epiphany of the Beloved is but one with her regime of tenderness."[3] The fragility and weakness of

---

[3] Emmanuel Levinas, *Totality and Infinity: An Essay on Exteriority*, trans. Alphonso Lingis (Pittsburgh: Duquesne University Press, 1969), p. 256. (The translation is modified in accord with present usage [e.g., *aimée* is here translated as "beloved woman"].—Tr.)

the beloved woman are the means by which the male lover can experience love of self as of a beloved who is powerless. Flesh of which he would remain the actual body.

Touching that which is not contained within the limits of his flesh, his body, the male lover risks an infinite outpouring into some dead being. He who has no connection to his own death puts the other at permanent risk of loss of self in the wrong infinity.

Touching can also place a limit on the reabsorption of the other in the same. Giving the other her contours, calling her to them, amounts to inviting her to live where she is without becoming other, without appropriating herself.

But does one who encounters only self in the beloved woman caress himself under the guise of a greater passivity? Adorning and inhabiting her with his own affects? If necessary, endowing her with some sense of touch as impersonal, a tactile *there is* adopted from his own subjectivity. Aporia of a tactility that cannot caress itself but needs the other to touch itself.

The threshold is still missing. The point of access to the most mucous part of the dwelling.

The abyss is circumscribed by the unavoidable alterity of the other. Its absolute singularity. Which should be protected prior to any positioning or affirmation of another transcendence? The transcendence of the "God" can help in the discovery of the other as other, a locus where expectation and hope hold themselves in reserve.

A dwelling place which becomes the matrix of the male lover's identity. Does she have no place anywhere? Hiding her dereliction in terror or irony, she calls for complicity with something other than profanation, animality, infancy. She calls—and sometimes in her dispersed state—to the feminine that she already is, secretly. Wanting to give herself over without giving up or violating her intimacy.

Modesty is not found on one side only. Responsibility for it should not belong to only one of the lovers. To make the beloved woman responsible for the secret of desire is to situate her also, and primarily in the place of the beloved man [*l'aimé*]—in his own modesty and virginity, for which he won't take ethical responsibility.

Would the task of the female lover be to watch over at least two virginities? Her own and the son's, to whom the male lover delegates the part of himself that is still virginal. A move toward interiority, of course. The male lover also seeks himself in this passage where he cannot cross the threshold from what is not yet to what is still in the future. Searching in infancy and animality for some moment whose obscure attraction remains insistent within himself. Call to an obscure night that is neither a return to immersion in the mother nor profanation of the beloved woman's secret, but the weight of his own mystery.

But, if some God obliterates respect for the other as other, this God stands as the guarantor of a deadly infinity. As a resource of life and love, the divine can only aid and further the fulfillment of the relation with the other. Provide the audacity of love. Encourage the risk of encountering the other with nothing held in reserve.

The fecundity of God would be witnessed in the uncalculating generosity with which I love, to the point of risking myself with the other. A loving folly that turns back the other's ultimate veil in order to be reborn on another horizon. Together, the lovers becoming creators of new worlds.

One should say, the lovers. Since to define the loving couple as a male lover and a *beloved woman* already assigns them to a polarity that deprives the female lover of her love. As object of desire, of the desirable, as call to the alterity of the night or the regression to need, the woman is no longer she who also opens partway onto a human landscape. She becomes part of the male lover's world. Keeping herself on the threshold, perhaps. Allowing the limits of her world, her country, to founder, to be swallowed up. But remaining passive within the field of activity of a subject who wills himself to be the sole master of desire. Leaving him, apparently, the whole of sensual pleasure, leaving him to a debasement without recourse to herself. What remains for him is reliance on the son as the continuation of his path.

Thus, the God, like the son, would serve as a prop in the ethical journey of man, who forgets to safeguard for the female lover the light of her return to self. He looks at her before plunging her into the night of his jouissance, his infantile or animal regression. But isn't it in the space between God and son that he takes her and annuls her as other? And renders her profane through his transcendence and relation to the divine?

Sensual pleasure would remain that which does not know the other. Which seduces itself, through her, to go down to the depths and return to ethical seriousness. Not coming face to face with an other who is responsible, especially for pleasure. But shirking this responsibility in the thoughtlessness of pleasure. An indifferent shore where he finds repose from ethical integrity?

Wouldn't the most terrible ethical demand be played out in that scene? Because it is a confrontation, here and now, with the mystery of the other. Because it is tied to a past and a future of incarnation. Modesty being a sign of an intimacy that demands, even begs for, a return. A supplication that calls wordlessly to reappear beyond immersion, in a light that has not yet been seen.

To give or give back to the other the possible site of his identity, of his intimacy: a second birth that returns one to innocence. A garment that isn't one, a kind of an envelopment that keeps continual watch over a space for birth—becoming other than a return to self. A becoming in which the other gives of a space-time that is still free. In which he re-entrusts me to a genesis that is still foreign to what has already taken place.

This gesture is more modest than the caress. A caress that precedes every caress, it opens up to the other the possible space of his respiration, his conception. Greeting him as other, encountering him with respect for what surrounds him—that subtle, palpable space that envelops each of us like a necessary border, an irradiation of our presence that overflows the limits of the body. Capable of more than the "I can" of the body itself.

This caress would begin at a distance. Tact that informs the sense of touch, attracts, and comes to rest on the threshold of the approach. Without paralysis or violence, the lovers would beckon to each other, at first from far away. A salutation that means the crossing of a threshold. Pointing out the space of a love that has not yet been made profane. The entrance into the dwelling, or the temple, where each would invite the other, and themselves, to come in, also into the divine.

Not divided into their alliances between highest and lowest, the extremes of day and night, but summoning these ultimate sites at the risk of union and fecundation of each by the other. A passage through the loss of the individual body, through the surrender of the "I can" that opens up a future without the sacrifice of the one to the other. Creation of love that does not abandon respect for the ethical.

This union does not ignore sensual pleasure; it sounds out its most plummeting and soaring dimensions. Not divided into elements belonging to different domains, the lovers meet as a world that each reassembles and both resemble. Inhabiting it and dressing it differently. The male lover's and the female lover's horizons being irreducible.

[207]

❦

The beloved woman—when called a child or an animal—is also she who holds the highest note. Whose voice carries the farthest, is the finest, and the strongest.

Her fall into the depths would mean that her voice was lost. Her song unheard. Her vocalism forgotten. The beloved woman would be mute or reduced to speaking in the spaces between the consonants of the male lover's discourse. She would be relegated to his shadow as his double, that which he does not yet know or recognize in himself, presenting itself to him under the guise of the beloved woman. Disguising for him the space of the present. An engulfment of his in-stance in the present, which clings to memory, and the song of the female lover. Which he sends down to the depths so that he can rebound into the transcendent. Manifested in and through writing. Absent and awaited in spirit. Whose voice would have been silent for a long time. A seriousness that is hard to maintain, which history would try to rediscover, re-uncover through the text.

Neither wanting nor knowing how to see himself in this body that he is no longer, the male lover would appear to himself in a female other, mystery of the site of his disappearance. In order to keep the secret, she must keep quiet, no song or laughter. Her voice would give her away. Reveal that she is not what the male lover thinks or searches for. That she is only a cover for what he is seeking, through and despite her.

Before parousia occurs, silence happens. A silence that rehearses oblivion and is only filled by music. There, the voice of the woman who sings and calls to the lover is still missing. It has been stifled by the noise of instruments and of nature running wild or abandoned to prostitution.

Unless she, too, disguises herself, in the guise of angels? Who perhaps have no sex? An interval that speaks between the bride and the spirit? Neither the one nor the other expressing themselves, unless it is through the mediation of the orders of the angels.

The expectation of parousia would also mean the death of speech between the sexual partners of the scene. Which foretells the terrible aspect of a new cosmic chaos and the disappearance of the gods. The hope of a new pentecost? Of the spirit's coming to the bride in the joy of a different union.

The feminine would remain in search of its cause and sought out as a cause, but never thought through as such. Always relegated to another kind of causality. At best, defined qualitatively. Women the adjectives or ornaments of a verb whose subject they can never be.

The logos would maintain itself between the verb and the substantive. Leaving out the adjective? A mediation between the act and its result. The place of attraction? In between loving and love would be the place of the beloved—man or woman. The one who is lovable. Approachable in his/her tenderness.

The two philosophical gestures would come down to grounding, unfolding, and surrounding that which founds itself: acting and constituting the substantive of the act. Closure of an age. The partly open would be remembered in the qualities of the beloved woman. Her already passive appearances or attributes? Over which she keeps watch, however, as they resist being taken up into substance.

Does the beloved woman's appeal convey a sense of that which has not yet solidified into the hardness of a name or noun or the seal of a signature? Between the act and the work would be situated that which reveals a future that the male lover understands not as the work of love but as the lightness of sensuality. As the repository of certain characteristics which the male lover does not retain when he is a beloved, the beloved woman's significance derives from this less than nothing, a substitution that does not disclose itself as such. She is brought into a world that is not her own so that the male lover may enjoy himself and gain strength for his voyage toward an autistic transcendence. In his quest for a God who is already inscribed but voiceless, does she permit him not to constitute the ethical site of lovemaking? A seducer who is seduced by the gravity of the Other but approaches the female other carelessly, he takes her light to illuminate his path. Without regard for what shines and glistens between them. Whether he wills it or not, knows it or not, he uses this divine light to illuminate reason or the invisibility of the "god."

In the meantime, he will have taken from the beloved woman this visibility that she offers him, which strengthens him, and will have sent her back to darkness. He will have stolen her gaze. And her song. Her attraction to a divine that becomes incarnate—in light, in the contemplation of the universe and the other. The divine revealed in those of its dimensions that are also accessible to the senses. Having already appeared and still to come, and which beauty would call to mind? A partial opening. A threshold. Also between past and future. The male lover steals her desire from her to adorn his world—which predates love—to spark his pleasure and aid his ascent following the lightness of a fulfillment that will not occur in the encounter between them. A union, or wedding, that is broken off at least twice. No "human" flesh is celebrated in that *eros*.

Failing to take into account his own limits, the male lover penetrates into flesh that he consumes and consummates without attention to the sacrificial gesture. He "takes communion" without benefit of rites or words. He is absorbed into nothing—unless it is his Other? Without detectable transition. Without a trace of this rape. If it were not for the exhaustion and suffering of the beloved woman, who is reduced to infancy, left to herself or to animal savagery.

Confounding the one and the other, bending them to the same logic, the male lover ignores the irreducible strangeness of the one and the other. Between the one and the other. He approaches the other to reduce it to that which is not yet human in himself. Sensual pleasure that does not take place in the realm of the human and will not be its creation. Neither ethical nor aesthetic.

When the female lover trusts the other beyond the limits of his possibilities, she is cast down and utterly forsaken. When she opens herself to the most intimate point of her being, to the most profound depths of her inwardness, but is not touched and returned to the most sublime part of herself, she is overcome by a night without end. Her invitation to inhabit this dwelling is a call for communion in the secret depths of the sensible realm and not for a defloration of herself as a woman.

The beloved woman's face illuminates the secret that the male lover touches on. Shining with a new light, bathed in a horizon that goes beyond intention, her face expresses what is hidden without disposing of it in a meaning. It is full of what cannot be said but is not nothing—thanks to the already and the not yet. A taking shape of matter that precedes any articulation in language. Like vegetative growth, animal anticipation, a sculptor's roughcast. An aesthetic matrix that has not yet produced results but is recognized as a prerequisite to the completion of all gestures.

The caress seeks out the not yet of the female lover's blossoming. That which cannot be anticipated because it is other. The unforeseeable nature of contact with otherness, beyond its own limits. Beyond the limits of its "I can." The irreducible nature of the other's presence, which is put off to a time always in the future, which suspends parousia indefinitely. The other, because it is still to come, would only maintain the male lover in his

[211]

love of self, as he makes himself beloved. He thus resigns from the woman's ethics, which is an opening of and to another threshold.

The act of love is neither an explosion nor an implosion but an indwelling. Dwelling with the self, and with the other—while letting the other go. Remembering while letting the other be, and with the world. Remembering the act not as a simple discharge of energy but for its characteristic intensity, sensation, color, and rhythm. The intensity would be or would constitute the dimensions of the dwelling, which is always in process. Never completed. Unfolding itself during and between the schedule of encounters.

If the beloved woman is relegated to infancy and animality, love has no dwelling. Nor does the male lover, who desires the ethical in a return to some Transcendent. Who bases this site on nostalgia for an inaccessible here and now of love and sensual pleasure?

Pleasure is never conceived as an instance of power in the act. It is said to be a way out, an exit from itself, as if tied to the instant, dispersing or rarefying our being—while overseeing an evasion. It is presented as an amputation of the being's ecstasy and not as a fulfillment that surpasses its destiny in the past and in the future. A liberation of being through the affective. Rather it is conceived as a break, a paroxysm whose promises cannot be kept, a disappointment and a deception in its internal becoming. Doomed to shame through its inability to measure up to the exigencies of need. Never up to what is expected of it. Never in the realm of the ethical.

Before the clamorous display of a presence that tells of nothing but its own emptiness, one should remain impassive in order to turn toward new values and horizons, without falling into the trap of a relapse into what has already been seen and known. The impatience of one who wants something else is not of the same register, musically, as the noise of one who cries out that he wants me not to want any longer. I am to want what he wants or to nourish myself on his desires, in that place where I can only do so at the cost of renouncing my incarnation.

An aggressive appeal by the other, who lets me know that he can no longer bear the suspension of his will. That he is hungry for my hunger. He is ready to destroy it in order to ignore the place where his hunger might take place—his appeal to the infinite, the unappeasable, the always more. He must bear its weight in separation, if I am to communicate with him in a dimension that guards the mystery of the absolute without abolishing it. In a demand for regressive nurturing, for example.

The lives of both the one and the other are at stake. A future is only possible if this respect for limits is admitted, also in the instant. If my hunger is not always turned back into uncertainty about the other's hunger. If he leaves me to the openness of my quest without absorbing me into his desire for nothing, unless it is to stifle what I am silently. In order to exist by himself?

One might as well say, to die? To produce, to produce himself in my place? This impossibility, which is both ridiculous from the start and insistent in its manifestations, can cut off my inspiration through its violence. For all that, however, he does not discover its source.

Forgetting that I exist as a desiring subject, the other transforms his need into desire. Desire for a nothing—the abolition of the other's willing, which would become a not-willing. Unless it is desire for a Transcendent—an Other of the same.

In this way, sensual pleasure finds itself set adrift, permanently. The distraction of transfiguration, transmutation, resurrection. An infinite substitution and spelling out of appearances, the masks falling without parousia? An illumination capable of being buried beneath displays, but not signifying a return to animality or infancy.

Does the male lover not impose upon the beloved woman that which he cannot see in himself? That which keeps him from becoming what he is, and from being able to encounter her, herself? Wrapping her up in what he cannot bear of his own identity, he secretly places her in the maternal position. A destiny, or maya, hidden in its identifying strata. A net which he cannot pass through again, which he imposes upon her, in order to rend it—figuratively. He discovers nothing. And if she surrenders as a child or animal, her finery fallen, the God becomes even more transcendent, inaccessible. Out of touch.

Might not the infinitesimal but impassable distance in our relation to death then be that which would take place in the touching of the female sex? Whence the assimilation of the feminine to the other? And the forgetting of a vital threshold—the tactile.

This locus of my concentration and of his opening out without futile dispersion constitutes a possible habitation. Turning back on itself and protecting me until the next encounter. A kind of house that shelters without enclosing me, untying and tying me to the other, as to one who helps me to build and inhabit. Discharging me from a deadly fusion and uniting me through an acknowledgment of who is capable of building this place. My pleasure being, in a way, the material, one of the materials.

Architects are needed. Architects of beauty who fashion jouissance—a very subtle material. Letting it be and building with it, while respecting the approach, the threshold, the intensity. Urging it to unfold without a show of force. Only an accompaniment? It only unfolds itself from being unfolded. It is in touch with itself from being touched while touching itself. It must be able to inhere. To continue to live in itself in order to live with. One must reach the heart of one's habitation in order to cohabit. This heart is always in motion and, at the same time, does not lack a dwelling. A qualitative threshold makes it possible for love to endure. For the lovers to be faithful? When they do not obey, the threshold wears out. The house of flesh, which lets them remember each other, call to each other—even at a distance—is destroyed.

Letting go and dwelling in the strength of becoming, letting the other go while staying contained and insistent, such is the wager that the female lover must make. Not holding back, but dwelling in that which wraps itself around a nonforgetfulness. That which is reborn, again and again, around a memory of the flesh. Flourishing again around what, in herself, has opened up and dispersed itself in sowings. Sowings that are fecund if she, the one who is unique, recalls this impossible memory. Is attentive to a time that is always consecrated to the depths. To drifting. To an infinite substitution.

There remain only the immemorial intrauterine abode and trust in some Other. Between blind nostalgia and ethical tension, the male lover loves and despises himself through the beloved woman—who is the beloved man. He attracts and rejects himself through this other, while he takes on neither infancy nor animality.

Is the memory of touching always disguised by senses that forget where they come from? Creating distance through a mastery that constitutes the object as a monument built in place of the subject's disappearance.

The memory of touching? The most insistent and the most difficult to enter into memory. The one that entails returning to a commitment whose beginning and end cannot be recovered.

Memory of the flesh, where that which has not yet been written is inscribed, laid down? That which has no discourse to wrap itself in? That which has not yet been born into language? That which has a place, has taken place, but has no language. The felt, which expresses itself for the first time. Declares itself to the other in silence.

One must remember this and hope that the other remembers. Lodge it in a memory that serves as its bed and its nest, while waiting for the other to understand. Make a cradle for him inside and out while leaving him free, and keep oneself in the memory of the strength that revealed itself, that acted.

But leaving free, giving an invitation to freedom, does not mean that the other wants it to be so. And lives in you, with you.

Far away, potentially. Avoiding encounters, approaches that convey the limits of the flesh. Remaining at a distance, in order to destroy the possibility of us?

A sort of abolition of the other, in the loss of the body's borders. A reduction of the other—even if it means consuming the flesh for the Other? Between the memory that preserves in expectation and respects the advent or the eventuality of the other and the memory that dissipates itself in assimilation, something is lacking—that memorial in which the flesh survives in its mobility, its energy, its place of inscription, its still-virginal power.

Must one have a certain taste? One that does not exist or inhere in any nourishment. A taste for the affective with and for the other. This taste that ought not to remain in an obscure nostalgia but rather ought to attend to that which always forgets itself. As impossible to gratify? Which does not exclude the enjoyment of whoever feels without wanting to absorb or re-solve. Between the body and the subtlety of the flesh—bridge or place of a possible encounter, unusual landscape where union is approached?

It is not a matter of the preciosity of a fetish or of the celebra-tory perfume of some sacrifice. Prior to any construction of words, any enshrinement or destruction of idols or even of tem-ples, something—not reducible to the ineffable aspect of dis-course—would keep itself close to the perception of the other in its approach.

The other cannot be transformed into discourse, fantasies, or dreams. It is impossible for me to substitute any other, thing or god, for the other—because of this touching of and by him, which my body remembers.

[216]

To each wounding separation, I would answer by refusing the holocaust while silently affirming, for myself and for the other, that the most intimate perception of the flesh escapes every sacrificial substitution, every assimilation into discourse, every surrender to the God. Scent or premonition between my self and the other, this memory of the flesh as the place of approach means ethical fidelity to incarnation. To destroy it is to risk the suppression of alterity, both the God's and the other's. Thereby dissolving any possibility of access to transcendence.